WITHDRAWN

PIERRE CARDIN
Making Fashion Modern

PIERRE CARDIN
Making Fashion Modern

Jean-Pascal Hesse
Pierre Pelegry
Foreword Jean Paul Gaultier

Flammarion

EXECUTIVE DIRECTOR
Suzanne Tise-Isoré
Style & Design Collection

EDITORIAL COORDINATION
Lara Lo Calzo

EDITORIAL ASSISTANCE
Virginie Picat
Loïc Derrien

GRAPHIC DESIGN
Clément Prats

TYPESETTING
Joseph Tsai

CAPTIONS
Karine Huguenaud

TRANSLATION FROM THE FRENCH
Inge Laino

COPY EDITING AND PROOFREADING
Clodagh Kinsella

PRODUCTION
Élodie Conjat

COLOR SEPARATION
Frédéric Claudel, Paris

PRINTING
Printer Trento, Italy

Simultaneously published in French as *Pierre Cardin, Mode Mythe Modernité*.

© Éditions Flammarion, Paris, 2022
English-language edition
© Éditions Flammarion, Paris, 2022

All rights reserved. No part of this book may be reproduced in any form or by any means, electronic, photocopy, information retrieval system, or otherwise, without written permission from Éditions Flammarion.

Éditions Flammarion
82, rue Saint-Lazare
75009 Paris
editions.flammarion.com
@styleanddesignflammarion

22 23 24 3 2 1
ISBN: 978-2-08-028189-0
Legal Deposit: 09/2022

Front cover:
Model Celia Hammond by Norman Parkinson in a Pierre Cardin outfit for *Queen* magazine, February 27, 1962.

Page 2:
Pierre Cardin in his early days, in his office at 118 Rue du Faubourg Saint-Honoré in Paris.

Facing page:
A visionary couturier and ingenious creator, Cardin dedicated his life to culture. He readily invested in the performing arts and even produced a few records.

Contents

DEAR MONSIEUR CARDIN *Jean Paul Gaultier*	8
PREFACE *Jean-Pascal Hesse*	11
PREFACE *Pierre Pelegry*	12
A CHILD'S DREAM	16
THE HAND OF FATE	20
DECISIVE ENCOUNTERS: JEAN COCTEAU AND CHRISTIAN DIOR	28
HAUTE COUTURE: FIRST COLLECTION	44
118 RUE DU FAUBOURG SAINT-HONORÉ	78
A WORLD OF INSPIRATION	96
THE CARDIN UNIVERSE	118
THE NEW STAR OF MEN'S FASHION	150
THE 1960s	170
JEANNE MOREAU, THE MUSE	188
A SELF-MADE MAN	198
A MAN OF CULTURE	210
THE COSMOCORPS ERA	218
ACKNOWLEDGMENTS	251
INDEX	252
PHOTOGRAPHIC CREDITS	254

Contact sheet by Roland de Vassal, photographer and friend of Pierre Cardin. An improvised photography studio was set up in the salons of 118 Rue du Faubourg Saint-Honoré in March 1960.

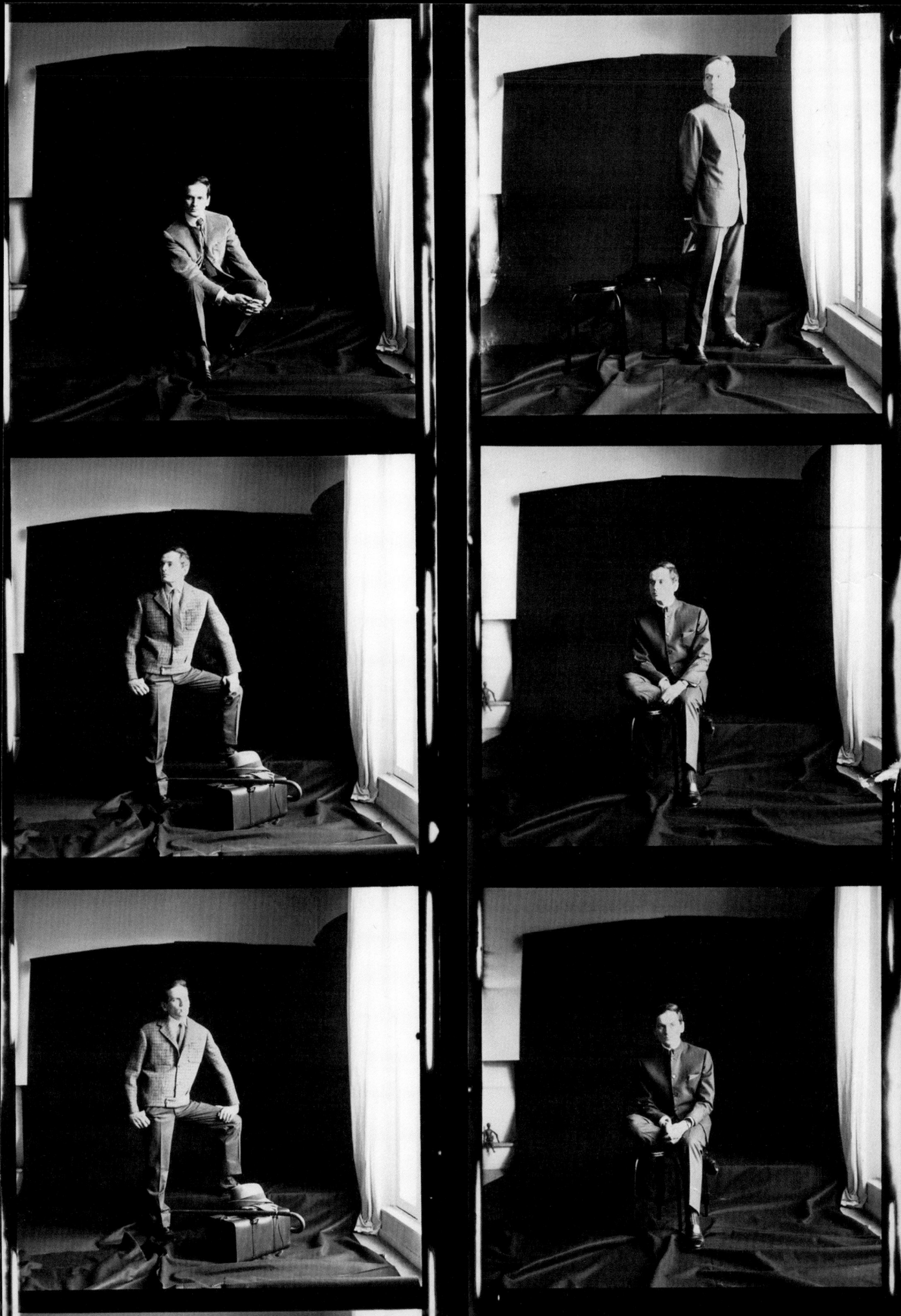

Dear Monsieur Cardin,

You taught me freedom.
From my teenage years, you were my favorite designer, due to your incredible creativity.
It all started on April 24, 1970, my eighteenth birthday. On that day, I received the best birthday present ever. A few weeks earlier, I had sent you some sketches and they convinced you to consider working with me, even though I had no training in fashion whatsoever.
My experience with you was my education in fashion, my bible. Your studio was a door thrown open onto the wide world. All sorts of nationalities were there: Indian, Japanese, Dutch, American, Argentinian, to name a few. It was the essence of cosmopolitanism. If you played the role of a worldwide ambassador for France, your studio was itself an embassy of the world in France.
Some of my sketches really caught your attention, including some absolutely fantastical—not to say downright unwearable—sunglasses. Sunglasses with a mirror logo, sunglasses with sun rays embedded in the lenses (talk about practical!), or even XXL mask-sunglasses which went all the way down beneath the chin!
At Pierre Cardin, anything was possible.

You were the first true designer of men's fashion, with more sensuous silhouettes, more daring suits, which the Beatles loved. Their famous suits with collarless jackets were your work.
You were the first great designer to make ready-to-wear, despite the disapproval of your conservative counterparts.
You were the first to propose fashion shows set to music by contemporary composers, like Pierre Henry, with his *La Messe du Temps Présent*, or Jean-Michel Jarre.
You were the first to turn your name into an empire, with licensing deals in countless fields, when versatility was sometimes frowned upon.
You were the only designer who took the helm of his own fashion house, acting as creator, manager, accountant, press agent, master tailor, master cutter, and *premier d'atelier* with unmatched savoir-faire. You knew how to make seemingly simple and minimal things—which is in fact the hardest to do—as well as create kinetic effects in black and white that imitated motion. You were in perfect step with the spirit of the times and did what every creator must do: capture the zeitgeist, the desires and aspirations of a generation.
Included among all the barriers you broke down were those of time itself.
I saw you for the last time just a few months before you died, for the screening of a documentary showing you hard at work—at ninety-eight years old!
You continue to transcend the boundaries of time, leaving in your wake a tremendous fashion legacy.
For all of this, I thank you.
Thank you, Monsieur, for giving me a chance and allowing me to fulfill my dream.
Thank you for teaching me to play and have fun, and for being an example of freedom.
Thank you, Monsieur, for these beautiful wings that you have given me.

Jean Paul Gaultier

The iconic cocktail dresses from the 1966 collection worn with felt riding hats. Jean Paul Gaultier drew inspiration from this design for the pointed-breast corset dress that he created in 1983, and that Madonna wore in 1990 for her "Blond Ambition" tour. Photograph by Yoshi Takata.

Preface

On the wall of my office on Avenue de Marigny is a photograph of Pierre Cardin taken by Roland de Vassal. It's been hanging there for a little over twenty-seven years. It seems to watch me, and I feel in Cardin's gaze the strength of his talent, his daring. He's there: my boss, but also a creator, a visionary.

Pierre passed away in December 2020, but I still sense his presence—irreplaceable—everywhere in this house dedicated to couture, art, and trade. A little like a wave, when the tide starts to pull out, dates, events, looks, and words intermingle. Memories that have enriched me in a thousand ways come flooding back. Today I am still in charge of the group's public relations, but I fear that "Pierre Cardin" remains more familiar as a brand name than that of a man.

Who would have believed for a second that this little boy from a modest and precarious background, who arrived from Italy at the age of two, in the 1920s, with his parents and one of his brothers, would go on to become an ambassador of fashion, creativity, haute couture, ready-to-wear, and the arts?

As a young man, Pierre didn't take long to realize he was born under a lucky star. He thought and breathed couture, fabrics, exceptional clothes. A unique, difficult, and demanding figure, he was determined to penetrate the world of fashion and never stopped believing in himself.

I joined the company in my thirties, somewhat by accident. The fashion world was uncharted territory for me. Pierre taught me a lot by giving me a lot. He was a public figure, with his impeccable dress sense, his undeniable charisma, and that allure which he never for a moment lost. Encounters with the likes of Jean Cocteau, Christian Dior, Luchino Visconti, and Jeanne Moreau were decisive for him. He may have lived in an ivory tower, but he loved nothing so much as intimate conversation around the table, when time ceases to count and talk cedes to memories, meetings, moments, emotions. He would delight us with tales of his travels. For years we had dinner together two or three times a week, with Yoshi Takata and Pierre Pelegry. He loved to talk. In writing this, I would like to offer my own account of my time with him.

Pierre Cardin reigned over fashion and couture for seven decades. At times, his appetite for glory and recognition threatened to compromise his reputation for excellence and luxury. Did he allow himself too much poetic license? Was he too much of a jack-of-all-trades? No matter. It's the journey of an exceptional man, an ingenious creator, that is the subject of this book. The pages that follow offer a glimpse of his beginnings, his key encounters, his brushes with fate, his friendships, and his ceaseless desires.

Jean-Pascal Hesse

Pierre Cardin
in his office. Photograph
by Roland de Vassal,
October 1957.

Preface

I met Pierre Cardin in 1996 when, as a young graduate, I had just finished my military service. He offered me the chance to join his team—and so it was that I discovered the brand universe of this self-taught man, an avant-garde and visionary designer who was always ahead of his time. It was a double opportunity for me: a chance to observe the creativity of this personality who never ceased to reinvent himself by tirelessly revisiting fashion; and to learn from a real iconoclast who always remained true to himself.

Pierre Cardin was a free man, unfettered by convention, detached and radical in spirit. He always encouraged me to look at things from a less conventional, more personal, angle. He knew how to capture and render the zeitgeist with his forward-looking creations: clothes with a timeless look and instantly iconic style. To him, style was the hallmark of a true designer.

Reformer of haute couture and pioneer of ready-to-wear, Pierre embodied modernity and remained one of the only truly independent fashion designers, all the while building an empire. From him I learned self-confidence, independence of spirit, audacity, and a strength of character resistant to the judgement of others. The first couturier to launch a menswear collection, he also passed on to me a taste for elegance—the kind that never goes out of style.

Pierre knew how to surround himself with key personalities such as André Oliver, his hugely talented designer-friend, and Maryse Gaspard, a model-muse who became the director of the couture department, and is still loyal to the house today. The artist Yoshi Takata, whom he met in 1954, also played a very important role in his life, taking him to Japan in 1957. They would work together for more than fifty years, until Pierre's death. A passionate photographer, Takata documented the Paris of the 1960s through the eyes of an emancipated woman, immortalizing the artists, writers, and celebrities of the time, as well as Cardin's creations: a vibrant witness to, and faithful supporter of, an ever-reinvented oeuvre.

Pierre was a man deeply in love with culture. As a patron of the arts, he was the first to program the then-unknown young American theater producer Bob Wilson with his play *Prologue to Deafman Glance*, at the Espace Cardin, in 1971; as well as the work of Claude Régy, Pier Paolo Pasolini, and Jean-Louis Barrault. Pierre also acquired the Marquis de Sade's castle in Lacoste, in the Luberon region of France, where he founded a theater and classical music festival.

When Pierre became the owner of Maxim's, he entrusted me with giving the restaurant back its soul by welcoming people from the worlds of art, fashion, and entertainment, reviving its authentic Art Nouveau decor, and restoring its prestige. I wanted to capture in book form the images and magical talent of this man to whom I wish to pay tribute by sharing Yoshi Takata's photographs.

I extend my warmest thanks to Jean-Pascal for giving me the opportunity to participate in this book.

Pierre Pelegry

Yoshi Takata was a faithful friend of Pierre Cardin and worked closely with him. The two met in 1954. Close to major humanist photographers such as Boubat, Brassaï, Cartier-Bresson, and Doisneau, she was the official photographer of the Pierre Cardin fashion house.

Making Fashion Modern

Pierre Cardin in 1956. Photograph by Yoshi Takata. The young designer's eyes and gestures exude ambition, will, and determination.

A CHILD'S DREAM

On a freezing winter's day in 1924, a couple and their two young children were waiting for the train. The setting was the Mestre railway station in Venice—less famous than the Lido or the legendary Piazza San Marco but set opposite the Grand Canal and the San Simeone Piccolo church. The man carried two large suitcases and a backpack, the woman a large knapsack and, in her arms, a toddler, Pietro. Cesar, their four-year-old son, was at their side. The parents had decided weeks earlier to leave the village of San Biago di Callalta, located about twenty-five miles from Venice, in search of a better life abroad.

This region of Italy was still very rural; industry was in its nascent stages. The couple owned silkworm farms, vineyards, horse-drawn carriages, and ice boxes (hard-working men would go to the Dolomite mountains to get blocks of ice and bring them down to the valley to sell to butchers or hospitals). At the dawn of the twentieth century, the living was tough, and people had to earn their daily bread by the sweat of their brow.

Little Pietro, the last of thirteen children, would long remember those grape fields, those rural landscapes. The boy had to stand on his tiptoes to touch the bunches of fruit and pick a few mouthfuls to eat.

The Great War had just ended. Between 1915 and 1918, Italy paid dearly for its part in the conflict, and Austria-Hungary was no more. This region in the north-east of the country had suffered from the clashes between the Austro-Hungarian Empire and the monarchy of Piedmont-Sardinia, and still bore the scars of fighting. It's worth remembering that the Veneto region had only become fully integrated into Italy in 1918. The Habsburg Empire had disappeared with the treaties of Trianon and Saint-Germain—and, with it, Austro-Hungarian rule.

The Cardini family had always lived in this province of Veneto. Alessandro, the father, was the eldest of four brothers. Maria, the mother, came from Salgareda, where her family raised horses. Legend has it that she was the assistant of a Montenegrin singer during her youth. Enlisting at the front in the seventy-second infantry regiment, in 1915, Alessandro had asked Maria to take refuge with his siblings in Catania, Sicily, to escape the bombing. In 1916, after a trying journey when

Pierre Cardin as a boy, shortly after his arrival in France. This photograph was taken in 1928 in Saint-Étienne, where his family had taken refuge from Italian fascism.

she had almost perished at sea during a storm caused by the eruption of Stromboli, she settled in an inn on Via Etnea. When the war was over, the family returned to San Biagio to find their house destroyed and the land devastated. One of Maria's brothers, who owned farms, offered them refuge in a farm building. The return was difficult, not least because of political turmoil and the country's gradual slide into crisis. The Fascist movement was gaining ground: Italian factions sought to seize power by any means. In October 1922, the March on Rome ushered in Benito Mussolini as prime minister. Repression was fierce; opponents hunted down. Italians left their homelands for the north of the peninsula or moved to the United States, South America, France, Belgium, Germany and elsewhere.

At that time, France, which had suffered many casualties during the Great War, was looking for hands to help rebuild the country. From Avignon, Giovanna, Pietro's sister, twenty years his elder, wrote to her family. In her letters, she spoke of France and its grand ideals. Pietro's aunts and uncles had left for South America and his parents agreed to leave with their youngest children, entrusting one of their eldest, Erminio, to an aunt, who would take care of his education in Italy. They sold a few acres of land, furniture, and everyday objects, and decided, with their war indemnity, to leave their hamlet of Sant'Andrea di Barbarana for Venice, then France—more specifically, Grenoble. The journey was long and uncomfortable. Thinking ahead, the couple sought to protect their toddler from the cold and bought him a coat in a store near the station. It was white, warm, and cozy. Pietro was two and a half years old, and for the rest of his life he would remember the softness of the fabric, the pleasure of feeling it wrapped around him, of being warm, even of running his hand over it. He would often evoke, with emotion, the memory of this sensation. A hand and a fabric: an encounter.

To get to Grenoble, the train had to pass through the Mont-Cenis tunnel. With the noise of the locomotive on the rails, the whistles and screeches and acrid black smoke rising, it is no wonder that the little boy was petrified. Nine miles of anguish and tears. Then Modane, France, and new skies unfurling. Little Pietro calmed down and was about to embark on a new life. The mists of Friuli-Venezia Giulia ceded to the welcoming French Alps. Exit Pietro Cardini, enter Pierre Cardin. The fairytale had begun.

For a child born in Italy, living in France at that time was like living in a utopia or storybook. However, things were far from easy. In Italy, the Cardini family had enjoyed a small degree of affluence, but their life now was more modest. Their first children were pampered, but for the last-born, everything was very precarious. In addition, the elder daughters—Rita, Alba, Teresa, and Palmira—had also had to flee, settling in La Tour du Pin, where they lodged with nuns. They found jobs in the factories at Dickson, a company created in 1918, specializing in the manufacture of coated fabrics.

The young immigrant Pierre soaked up French language and culture. School helped him to integrate but he saw, with the all-seeing eyes of a child, that his parents were old and foreign. Because of his advanced age, Pierre's father struggled to make ends meet doing odd jobs. He was, in turn, a laborer and a metal worker at the Crozet-Fourneyron factory in Chambon-Feugerolles. He never held a steady job. The family lived near Grenoble and La Tour du Pin. Pierre's parents were mild-mannered. They read books, enjoyed discussions, and shared the housework. These attitudes were to leave their mark on the boy, who saw in them a form of society where the sexes were more or less equal, and gender roles less rigid. A family where it was not strange to see the father wash the dishes or sweep the floor. It was the time of the Great Depression of the 1930s, there was no such thing as unemployment benefits, and individual solidarity was the only thing one could hope for. But for Pietro, daily life was an uphill battle. He was called *macaroni*, a derogatory term for immigrant Italians. Hurt, offended, and stigmatized by the name, the boy's scars ran deep. Reality in France did not live up to the country's lofty ideals: Pierre was a victim of xenophobia.

Pierre and his family next lived in Saint Clair de la Tour, two miles from La Tour du Pin, where his father was employed at the Dickson Walrave rope factory. He would always remember the spinning mill and the factory, the smell of the apples gathered by his parents for the winter, and the sacks of nuts. In 1931, on the recommendation of André, the eldest son, the family finally settled in Saint-Étienne, at 18 Rue de Firminy. This manufacturing city was steeped in industrial and working-class tradition. The Cardinis stayed there until 1939, when they moved to Rue Dard-Janin, in a small house owned by the city's civil hospices.

By this time, Pierre was seventeen. Already the memory of Italy had faded, the language of Molière replacing that of Dante. At school he became acquainted with the giants of French civilization: Gaulish chieftain Vercingetorix, Charlemagne, Joan of Arc, Louis XIV, Napoleon, Pasteur. At thirteen, the discerning adolescent formally requested naturalization. Enquiries were launched into his family's past, certificates of good conduct requested. Pierre was finally officially naturalized French at the same time as his parents and his brother César, on December 25, 1936. It was a major turning point in his life.

Pierre attended the local school in Saint-Étienne. He spoke French, thought in French, dreamed in French. Already he knew that he was irresistibly drawn to textiles, fabrics, and sewing. He wanted to "imagine shapes, create dresses, and dress women." It was also there that, armed with bits of fabric brought back from the factory by his sisters, he dressed the dolls of his young friends. One day, towards the end of his primary school education, the young Pierre Cardin was asked about his professional ambitions. To the age-old question "What do you want to be when you grow up?," he answered, simply: "A couturier."

But how to incorporate these activities into his life? Or vice versa? In the meantime, like all children of his age, Pierre enjoyed playing ball, and cops and robbers. He even became a scoutmaster. He would later admit that he liked to be on the side of order. He was a natural leader and happy to be in charge. These early social roles marked him for life.

By the summer of 1936, Pierre was still in Saint-Étienne and obsessed with getting a foothold in the world of couture. He spotted a tailoring store, run by Louis Bompuis, a local artisan, on Rue du Général Foy. He solicited him in different ways, selling himself as "the indispensable apprentice." The owner and his wife were running things alone and getting on in age. They took on the ambitious teen, a bit of a jack-of-all-trades, who played the piano and accompanied them on picnics, brightening their days as he fulfilled the role of a son or a nephew. Pierre learned the basics, the tools of the trade, observing and taking note of everything as he grew and bolstered his confidence.

THE HAND OF FATE

In May and June of 1940, France was falling apart, the world flipping on its axis. Amid the turmoil, Pierre Cardin longed to go to Paris, dreaming of the city's bright lights and clamor. After saying goodbye to his parents, he set off on his bicycle one summer's day. The bike, which he had bought from the Manufacture d'Armes et Cycles, a cycle and sporting-gun company in Saint-Étienne, featured balloon tires—a novelty at the time. Stopped in Moulins, just as he was about to cross the demarcation line between free and occupied France, he was interrogated by German soldiers. They were a little suspicious of this young man on wheels and transferred him to Vichy, to be interrogated by Gestapo officers. Quickly released, Pierre found himself all alone in the middle of a town where he knew no one.
But he was bold: a character trait that would always define him. Near the city park and the famous hotel housing the leaders of the new regime, the Mamby fashion house dazzled him with its window displays of mannequins, high fashion, and big dreams. Intimidated but impudent, the eighteen-year-old enquired about a job and was promptly hired by the owner, who saw his desire to work and be close to creativity, fine fabrics, and elegance. Blanche Popinat, the manager, and former head seamstress of Chanel, took him on for his fresh-faced looks and energy. It was an important step in Pierre's life—and, as proof of his attachment to the maison, a quarter of a century later he would buy back the place where it had all begun.
In the boutique-workshop, Pierre did a little bit of everything. During his time at Bompuis, in Saint-Étienne, he had been initiated into couture, but in Vichy there was a considerable advantage: the team directed by Blanche Popinat continued to work for the house of Chanel under the direction of Gabrielle Chanel, reproducing its patterns. The young apprentice knew that these particular garments were the fruit of much care and application, the sign of another world of clothing and fashion. He closely observed proceedings and learned the ropes.

"Elegance gives you style," proclaimed Pierre Cardin. The designer pictured during his early days in Paris, around 1950.

France now plunged into the occupation, was collaborating with the Nazi regime. Having lost touch with his family, the road ahead was lonely for the young Pierre. In February 1943, the German war machine was mobilizing men at all costs; the Eastern Front devouring the country's young soldiers. Industry, agriculture, and the railroads were short of manpower, and the Pétainist government in France succumbed to the occupiers' demands. Youths between the ages of seventeen and twenty-five were conscripted. Nearly six hundred thousand young Frenchmen were forced to work in Greater Germany, in the name of the *Service du Travail Obligatoire* (STO), an obligatory work scheme. Pierre Cardin had to go to Stettin, a production center for military equipment, and port that reverted to Poland after the war. His name appeared on the departure lists. Once again, luck was on his side and he was chosen, along

Pierre Cardin as an adolescent, photographed in 1938 in front of his parents' house in Saint-Étienne.

with one of his comrades, to work as an accountant for the Red Cross in Vichy. A stay in Pomerania could have changed the course of his life—and that of fashion history.

With his lucky star still shining, then, Pierre stayed in Vichy, to work with General Verdier at the Treasury of the General Delegation of the Red Cross. At the age of just twenty-one, he was assigned to the payroll department, managing the salaries of some eight hundred employees. Although he had taken evening classes in general accounting, Pierre had little taste for numbers. Nonetheless he learned the secrets of the balance sheet, operating accounts, tills and banking—all skills which would come in handy much later when he went into business in earnest. In addition, like many of his peers, he was a first-aid worker. Turning outwards, he learned solidarity and how to care for others, pivotal values and abilities which would aid him, on a daily basis, with the multiple tasks of his future life.

Vichy didn't have much to offer the local youth. After work, and before the curfew, they would try to forget about the rigors of war with parties, music, and dancing. They met in the woods and in barns or remote houses. Some went home to their families, while others joined the resistance, out of political conviction or rejection of the STO.

It was the time of the *zazous*, a subculture associated with flashy clothing and swing jazz that stood in open opposition to the war and forces of order. One evening in the spring of 1944, Pierre joined a handful of friends in Montluçon, fifty-six miles by bike from where he lived. They travelled in groups, unafraid of bombings, fights, or skirmishes—and the faster they pedaled, the faster they left the war and occupation behind them. Gathering in a kind of café-brasserie, at one point, a little out of breath, Pierre went to the restroom to freshen up. Suddenly, he heard a noise and the music stopped. There was shouting and the sound of chairs being jostled: the Milice! Faithful helpers of the Gestapo, these Frenchmen had been engaged by the group's leader Joseph Darnand from January 1943 onwards, and were simultaneously formidable and feared. They mercilessly hunted down Jews, STO draft dodgers, and Resistance fighters, putting their arrested "suspects" through hell, be it torture or other acts of violence. The men constituted a political police force in the service of French-style fascism. Pierre Cardin, once again, had a magnificent stroke of luck. Several of his friends were arrested and taken away for interrogation and abuse but he, mute with fear, hid in the restroom and narrowly escaped their fate.

It was a time of bombs, hunger, and cold. Sunday meals often consisted of stale bread and thin soup. A day's ration was a five-ounce piece of bread and a mint-flavored "Vichy" pastille: way too little for a young man, making Pierre a student in the school of hard knocks. But though things were bitterly hard, Pierre stayed put, exposed to the vagaries of wartime. His work was not unpleasant; he was at least allowed to send books and food to French POWs in the "Stalag" and "Oflag" war camps. Hardship only made him stronger; later he would say that all these trials made him aware of the obstacles of everyday life. Another milestone in these years of apprenticeship came in 1943, when he was sent to a youth camp, near Clermont-Ferrand, for nine months. He attended a management school and became a site foreman supervising a team of fifteen young men. The purpose of these mandatory projects was to promote "national values." What would remain with Pierre from the experience was a taste for being in charge, an awareness of the demands of organization, and a concern for group cohesion.

In the summer of 1944, the Allied forces liberated Paris and the specter of war dissipated. The Vichy regime, as well as the Red Cross' local operations, were dissolved. People fled, but Pierre, marked by a strong sense of duty, stayed until the bitter end. Eventually there were only three people left in his offices; the situation was dire. Pierre, too, felt that his life was elsewhere—namely Paris. He had no money and no contacts, and his conception of the work he wanted to do was still sketchy, but he knew one thing for certain: Paris would be the stage!

    At the same time, he often rubbed shoulders with the Countess of La Cambredette in the café of the Hotel de Surville. She was an elegant woman who liked to read people's fortunes. In November 1945, he asked her for a reading. He was burning to know: should he become an actor, a dancer, or a fashion designer? He needed advice and, anguished, he turned to her: "Madame, I have to go to Paris since the Red Cross has been dissolved. I would like to work somewhere in fashion, could you give me an address? Above all, give me a glimpse of what the future holds for me. I have sent many of my friends to you, but you have never agreed to see me." She drew the cards, looked at the lines on his palm and predicted: "It is extraordinary. In thirty years doing this, I have never seen a life as intriguing as yours. I see a tree and you climbing to ever greater heights, infinitely high. You will succeed brilliantly; you will have an exceptional career until the day you die. Your name will be known throughout the world. I see you in Australia, all over the world, in Sydney, precisely." To the one she affectionately called "petit Pierre," she promised a "success story," which would be all the more extraordinary since it would be that of a man who started from nothing and owed his rise solely to hard work and a creative mind.

But how could this dream possibly come true? Somewhat stunned and incredulous, Pierre wondered: how could a poor child, with no means to travel, go around the world? Nonetheless, he relished the unlikely prediction. Taking cautious steps, he dared to ford the river. Afterall, the fortune-teller was a woman of means, a Parisian, and full of goodwill. "Go see Monsieur Waltener, on Rue du Faubourg Saint-Honoré in Paris. He has special access to the Paquin house…he will welcome you with open arms."

Back then, Maison Paquin was the equivalent of Christian Dior or Yves Saint Laurent nowadays. Of course, the young man, still in a daze, was not yet aware of it. He knew only one thing: he couldn't leave for Paris fast enough. His destination: 82 Rue du Faubourg Saint-Honoré. Within a few days, Pierre had rid himself of his personal effects, given up his room, and snapped his small suitcase shut. He was ready!

    On November 17, 1945—a Saturday—Pierre climbed aboard a Red Cross truck. It's not hard to imagine the state of the roads, the difficulty of finding fuel in a country that was desperately trying to turn the page on the greatest war ever known. A fellow traveler who knew Paris well recommended a small, inexpensive hotel in the city center, on Rue Vivienne. Pierre had nothing to worry about; Monday noon, he was expected at the Red Cross headquarters in the eighth arrondissement of Paris.

    The next day, at 8 a.m. sharp, Pierre hurriedly got ready and set out in a daze for Rue du Faubourg Saint-Honoré. The way was long in this unknown city, and it was bitterly cold and snowing. Should he continue on an empty stomach or stop in a café for a hot drink? He decided to push on.

Pierre Cardin, on the right, at the time of his stay in Vichy during World War II. He worked as an accountant for the Red Cross until 1945.

His eyes drank in signs that were the stuff of dreams: Lanvin, Paquin, among others. Sensing that he was nearing his destination, Pierre passed a dapper fellow out walking his dog. The young *zazou* from the provinces, elegant in a rayon coat exchanged against ration stamps in Vichy, addressed the stranger.

"Hello Monsieur, I'm looking for number 82. Do you know if I'm close?"

"It's not far at all. Who are you going to see? Who are you looking for?"

"A friend, Monsieur Waltener. But I'm so cold…"

"I don't think I know you, but I'm Monsieur Waltener!"

The ground opened! Pierre felt unsteady on his feet. The first person he had ended up speaking to in Paris on this cold morning had turned out to be the very contact indicated by Madame de La Cambredette! They were in front of the Lanvin boutique, one of the best-known names in fashion. The Parisian invited the young man to "drink something warm… somewhere warm!" They entered a café and fell into conversation.

"Come and see me tomorrow morning. I'll call the Paquin house and give you the name of the person you're to meet. They'll take care of you."

Pierre left the bar brimming with confidence. There was no stopping fate. On Monday morning, November 19, he presented himself at Paquin, 3 Rue de la Paix. It was a major fashion house with a sterling reputation, employing over one thousand four hundred people: a world unto itself. He went to the reception desk. They were expecting him and took him to the atelier right away. He arrived like a swimmer ready to conquer the open seas. Diving in he felt, strangely, that he was in his element. He was ready for anything, would do anything, give anything. The dreamlike world of fashion permeated him to his very core and a kind of euphoria took hold of the young contender.

Pierre was determined to succeed and more. For him, to succeed meant having a position, being known and recognized, having his name in bright lights. He often said, "to succeed is to become someone." He believed it was his destiny to shake things up.

A Schiaparelli evening dress photographed in 1947 by Horst P. Horst. Pierre Cardin started working for Elsa Schiaparelli after the war, where he did odd jobs for a brief period in the couture workshop.

DECISIVE ENCOUNTERS: JEAN COCTEAU AND CHRISTIAN DIOR

Pierre immediately sensed a colossal gap between what he knew of life and work, and the world of Rue de la Paix. Jeanne Paquin had died in 1936, but Antonio del Castillo was now carrying on her spirit and her style. Vichy had been about "ordinary life"; now the young Pierre witnessed high-society women dropping by in the afternoon in Rolls Royces to discover the collections, escorted by uniformed drivers and maids, as in many movies of the 1950s. Women who, in one fell swoop, ordered fifty dresses and suits, as well as silk underwear and *negligees*—literally "slapdash" things in French: a misnomer if ever there was one. Pierre discovered the world of high fashion, envy, desire, appearance, distinction, elegance: everything that would form the basis of his artistic and commercial approach. The metamorphosis had begun and there was no turning back.

Once again, fortune smiled on the passionate young man. The atelier had just started collaborating with Jean Cocteau, who was assisted by the painter and decorator Christian Bérard and the costume designer Marcel Escoffier, an artist whose links to Auguste Escoffier, the king of chefs, Pierre Cardin liked to recall (Escoffier would

Pierre Cardin on his arrival in Paris, on Rue Royale. The eighth arrondissement was his favorite district.

Making Fashion Modern

PIERRE CARDIN AND JEAN COCTEAU

The meeting with Cocteau, decisive for the young Cardin, who was working for the Paquin fashion house at the time, happened in 1945 on the set of the mythical film *Beauty and the Beast*. The famous maison on Rue de la Paix had a staff of fourteen hundred men, and Pierre stood out for his enthusiasm and astute knowledge of the ins and out of the fashion world. He was entrusted with making the otherworldly costumes for Cocteau's film, later admitting to dreaming of them at night. His work with Cocteau continued afterwards, again under the aegis of Christian Bérard and Marcel Escoffier, for the artist's most memorable films, *The Eagle with Two Heads* (1948), *Ruy Blas* (1948), and *Orphée* (*Orpheus*, 1950).

go on to do costumes for Jean Delannoy, Luchino Visconti, Maria Callas and Franco Zeffirelli). André Paulvé—who would himself later work with René Clément and Sacha Guitry—was producing Cocteau's *La Belle et la Bête (Beauty and the Beast)*. Shooting was difficult and had already stretched to five months. Cocteau had fallen seriously ill, Jean Marais was in Switzerland and it was Pierre Cardin, of similar looks and height to the film's lead actor, who had a chance to shine, becoming Marais' body double. Cocteau and Bérard called him one day at the atelier and said, "Young man, can you try on this costume? You have more or less the same build as Jean." Honored, Pierre complied. His skills were also put to good use in making the costume, and he devised a system of straps to hold the mask of the "beast" in place. He later liked to say: "At that moment, I became the first male model in Paris." Fashion shows and exhibitions followed one after another. The costumes were magnificent, the materials a sheer pleasure to behold. Luck was on Pierre's side yet again. He who wanted to penetrate the worlds of fashion and cinema had killed two birds with one stone. He felt with all his soul that he was living a real fairytale and was determined to exploit it to the full. Not only did he wear Jean Marais' costumes, he also wore those of Michel Auclair, playing Belle's brother, Ludovic. In the afternoons, meanwhile, he often worked with Cocteau himself, or with Bérard or Marcel Escoffier, whom he befriended. Pierre would often say that his beginnings creating costumes for the art world or for haute couture resembled a kind of dream. The clothes the team designed together were wonderful. His fantasies were coming true in this period of post-war reconstruction.

At that time, Cocteau was the major Paris player. His appearances at premieres set the tone. He was an urbane and benevolent man; his *Beauty and the Beast* was a triumph and he went on to direct *L'Aigle à deux Têtes (The Eagle with Two Heads)* and *Œdipe-roi (Oedipus the King)*. Pierre, the young fashion prodigy, continued to discover this impressive artistic milieu. In Bérard's apartment on Rue Casimir-Delavigne, he was amazed by the profusion of drawings, paintings, sketches, and projects. He spoke of Bérard in these terms: "He took a paintbrush, a sheet of paper… and improvised! It was a display of pure virtuosity." At the same time, Pierre understood the subtle importance of connections and of chance. He knew how important it was to be devoted, mobile, available, and adaptable. His lucky star watched over him, and he continued to advance. Oftentimes, chance encounters make or break lives.

In 1946, on Cocteau's advice, Pierre tried his hand at the theater, enrolling in the Cours Simon, an acting school. He took badly to the sense of "servitude" implied in the work of an actor; he was too independent to perform roles and yearned for freedom—eventually dropping out. After nine months, having gained in confidence, he left Maison Paquin for Schiaparelli. Elsa Schiaparelli, Italian like him, was something of a provocateur. The young apprentice couturier nonetheless felt cramped, staying only a few months before resigning. What he really wanted was to enter the great house of Lucien Lelong on Avenue Matignon. He learned that the company, financed by Marcel Boussac, was in danger of changing hands. The great entrepreneur in the textile and equestrian worlds, considered at that time the richest man in Europe, hesitated for a time between relaunching an established fashion house with Lucien Lelong and Christian Dior at the helm, or creating a new one, headed only by the latter. After giving it some thought, he invested sixty million francs in Dior and launched the eponymous fashion house on Avenue Montaigne.

Jean Cocteau and Jean Marais in the late 1930s. Pierre Cardin was noticed by the poet while he was designing the costume for the *Beauty and the Beast* at Paquin.

Always on the lookout for opportunities, Pierre, who was beginning to build up a network, had long admired Lucien Lelong, who would come to be remembered in France for his lithe, modern silhouettes. Incidentally, a few years later, he would also become the first to imagine luxury ready-to-wear, envisaging a complete line uniting clothes, accessories, and perfumes, and thus creating a fashion range with an aesthetic, industrial and commercial dimension.

Pierre ultimately approached Christian Dior through his friend, the writer Philippe Hériat of the Académie Goncourt, to whom he remained close until his death. This bourgeois Norman, son of a family of industrialists, reassured him. Shortly before the opening, they had this candid exchange:

"I'd like to work with you."

"We'd love to have you! Come in three months' time to Avenue Montaigne. We'll work together."

"I'll be there!"

And so it came to pass.

Pierre now had a foot in the door at Dior. He appreciated the great man's lively spirit, his genius for elegance and aesthetics. The forty-one-year-old creator, erudite and cultured, also held his young counterpart in high esteem, and ended up propelling him to the forefront of the fashion scene. Pierre was the first employee to arrive, early in the morning of November 18, 1946. At number 30, the hôtel particulier was empty, devoid of furnishings. The house on Avenue Montaigne would only be inaugurated on December 16. The opening was a messy affair: works were still in progress, staff were being recruited, silhouettes created, and the teams on site were struggling to get it all done on time. They needed everything: irons, telephones, stools, fabrics. Pierre, a vital part of this operation, bought the first iron with his own money and welcomed his fellow workers. Work could now begin; the ship had lifted anchor.

The collection scheduled for completion in February 1947 was well underway. Christian Dior himself was running the show; it was he who imagined and designed the dresses and other models. His teams took over the relay with Raymonde Zehnacker, Mizza Bricard and Marguerite Carré directing the way. The lead tailor was none other than Pierre Cardin. Organized and managerial, Dior surrounded himself with a show and client manager, an administrative and financial director, and an advertising manager. Pierre, who spent money liberally, drank it all in, neglected nothing and took a mental note of everything. He knew that all this information would serve him well one day.

The young Pierre Cardin worked as first studio assistant under the supervision of Marguerite Carrée, Christian Dior's right-hand womanand technical director. Between them, the two were the pillars of the fledgling fashion house.

It was here that Pierre would acquire a core value—elegance and the means to achieve it: a lesson that would never leave him.

Dior knew what he wanted, but was of a volatile nature, regularly changing his mind. Co-workers, often of tremendous talent, came and went. While Pierre knew how to do everything—cut, sew, design, make a dress—Dior was dependent on the pattern-cutters and certain other employees to achieve his visions.

Above:
Jean Marais and Josette Day in *Beauty and the Beast* costumes designed by Christian Bérard and made by Paquin. Bérard's assistant, Pierre Cardin, made many of the costumes and masks for the film.

Right:
Jean Marais, for whom Pierre Cardin, thanks to his similar build, stood in for, while the beast and the prince's costumes were being fitted.

PIERRE CARDIN AND CHRISTIAN DIOR

Pierre Cardin often said, "It is to Christian Dior that I owe my sense of taste and elegance." For his part, Christian Dior, who openly admitted his attachment to "petit Pierre", as he called him, said, "Artists like Pierre Cardin are the future of haute couture." From the three years he spent with his master and mentor, the young Cardin learned precision, discipline, and high standards: qualities that would allow him to take his rare virtuosity to great heights. With his many talents, in 1947 Cardin participated in the design of the *Bar* jacket and the launch of the New Look, a revolutionary collection that brought international renown to Dior.

Christian Dior in the middle of a game of Patience. Christian Bérard appears in the background. Photograph by Louise Dahl-Wolfe, Fleury-en-Bières, 1947.

Pierre's opinion of this unmatched but indecisive designer was clear. He, the young man in a hurry, the "Captain of Gascony," to quote *Cyrano de Bergerac*, dreamed big. He defined himself as a warrior, an adventurer. He longed to upend codes and conducts. He observed this patrician, puffed up with the elegance of the aesthete, with the hungry look of a *ragazzo*, or Italian upstart. In other words, Pierre was looking for true fashion, to inject the soul into garments and allow the wearer to express their essence. He would, however, also say of Dior that he "transformed the hardships of life and the difficulties of the textile industry."

Paquin, Schiaparelli, Dior…a trinity of prestigious names coming at decisive stages in the early days of Pierre's life in fashion. The course of that life continued inexorably. The great creator lost his mother in 1948, while his father, Alessandro, died eleven years later, in 1959. Luckily, he had been there to witness his son's first successes and to receive a bottle of the latter's first perfume. The cathedral of Saint-Charles-Borromée in Saint-Étienne was packed at his funeral. Many had come in the hopes of seeing the prodigal son. Cardin's parents were laid to rest together in the cemetery of Montmartre, in Saint-Étienne, where their daughter Amélia had preceded them in 1935, at the age of twenty-two. Pierre never spoke about this sad event or about the solitude of his childhood.

Christian Bérard and his dog during a rehearsal of Jean Giraudoux's *The Madwoman of Chaillot*, Théâtre de l'Athénée, Paris, 1945. Cardin was an admirer of the great decorator and artist. He often visited him in his stuudio on Rue Casimir-Delavigne. Photograph by Boris Liptnitski.

Making Fashion Modern

During the occupation, the French economy was in a shambles. There was a lack of raw materials, the black market thrived, and levies were high. The top couturiers had to push the boundaries of creation, turning to new materials and inventing novel techniques. Haute couture had to adapt to the demands of the new climate but this did not tarnish the influence and prestige of French high fashion. When France was liberated, a new style was born, more in tune with the demands of women. France entered a thirty-year period known as the "Trente Glorieuses," when luxury, aesthetics and beauty once again took their rightful place after a time of violence and anxiety. On December 1, 1949, the last ration stamps for sugar, gasoline, and coffee disappeared. A page had truly been turned! Although haute

Christian Dior sketches a silhouette with a cinched waist, from the *Corolle* line. Photograph by Willy Maywald, 1948.

couture was not a priority, fashion was an economic and artistic sector very much linked to the image of France, and the stakes were high.

This was the era when Dior first created a collection replete with luxurious materials. As he described it: "We were just emerging from an impoverished era, lean times marked by an obsession with ration stamps and clothing coupons. Naturally, my vision took the form of a reaction against that poverty" (*Dior by Dior: The Autobiography of Christian Dior*, V&A Publishing, 2015).

Up in the attic, a faithful band was working around the clock on the first collection. It had to be an unforgettable event. On February 12, 1947, the house of Christian Dior, with its first fashion show, turned post-war fashion on its head. It was nothing less than a revolution. The "New Look" would sweep away old traditions in a single stroke.

The expression, still famous, represented a watershed moment. Later, Carmel Snow, the editor-in-chief of *Harper's Bazaar*, reprized it: "It's quite a revolution, dear Christian! Your dresses are wonderful, they have such a new look!"

It was widely agreed that this landmark collection put Europe back on the fashion map. Not easily forgotten, it would bring industry and trade back to the so-called "Old Continent" and remain one of the great events of the post-war period. All this is yet more remarkable as the fabrics of the time were of a mediocre quality when compared to those that were produced ten years later. The war was still weighing heavily on the industry.

In the aftermath of the occupation, Dior restored to fashion the right to dream and to women that of dressing to please. Pierre was embarking on a magnificent journey.

The *Corolle* line had its roots in the curves of flowers, and the 8 silhouette stood out thanks to its pinched waist and rounded forms, reminiscent of the shape of the number. If wartime had seen women's hemlines rise it was primarily due to the constraints and shortages of the period. Now that was over, hemlines fell. Dresses revealed no more than forty centimeters of calf, waistlines were slimmed down, shoulders remodeled, and the chest rounded out. At this time, fashion became a social affair and made an astonishing entry into everyday life — a real turning point in post-war society.

Europe was doing its best to turn its back on war, deprivation, and death. The world of fashion and haute couture began to mutate, setting out on what would be a long road. Pierre embodied the soul of the new collection. Obsessed with fashion, he lived only for the elegance of dresses, of life, of people.

The *zazous* still set the pace of fashion at the time. Boys sported long and loose jackets with sloping shoulders; their pants were short with big turn-ups. As for the girls, they carried bags with very long shoulder straps and wore tartan skirts, very short, with very long jackets.

Profoundly, even excessively talented, Pierre mastered designing, cutting, and stitching. Very quickly he could create a piece from start to finish. He did everything, he was everything. His presiding goal: to seek out a new form, or new forms plural.

Pierre was already successful — even very successful — and popular too. He thought of himself as the golden boy of the times. He still remained at 82 Rue du Faubourg Saint-Honoré, one of the most famous addresses in Paris' eighth arrondissement, next door to the Élysée Palace, home to the president of France.

However, a sordid story of copied models came to plague this man who was in such a rush to rise to the top. A pattern cutter from Dior was accused of theft, Pierre trusted him entirely, and quite naturally took his defense. But to take someone's defense is to become an accomplice! It was a very busy time, and everyone, including Pierre, was working around the clock. It was not uncommon for employees not to go home at night; weekends were days like any other. Disgusted that his integrity was being called into question, the young designer turned to Dior himself and to his general manager. "Since you no longer trust me, I must leave the company," he said. This upset Christian Dior, who replied, "You know, it's a logic of suspicion. You belong here, you know how much I appreciate you... You must stay!" They did everything to keep Pierre from leaving, but the couturier's pride was wounded. After three years of complete and total commitment, Pierre left the house of Dior. He had come to realize that it is better to be number one at home than number two somewhere else, even if that somewhere else is Dior. He had to make a decision: should he become a dancer? An actor? Do something in the field of fashion? Better an egg today than a hen tomorrow! He had just worked for three fashion houses in a row and felt that he had enough contacts to do something on his own. He had worked hard, learned a lot, and saved a lot too, something he learned from his early days, when he was no stranger to hardship. Etched in his memory were the sensations provoked by the fabric of that little white coat of his childhood, somewhere between pleasure and security.

Left:
Pierre Cardin (left), the first studio assistant at Dior, Avenue Montaigne, 1947.

Facing page:
Sketch by Christian Bérard for the *Bar* jacket from the *Corolle* line. Features the *Bar* jacket, woven straw hat, fitted jacket in silk shantung, slim shoulders and underlined chest, long finely pleated skirt.

Pages 40–41:
On February 12, 1947, Christian Dior presented his first haute couture Spring–Summer collection at 30 Avenue Montaigne, revolutionizing fashion. The *Bar* jacket became a legend and ensured the immediate success of the "New Look." Photograph by Pat English.

Pages 42–43:
Backstage at the same show, with Dior's collaborator and muse Mizza Bricard in the foreground. Photograph by Eugene Kammerman.

40

Making Fashion Modern

HAUTE COUTURE: FIRST COLLECTION

What is striking about Pierre Cardin's journey is the way that fate constantly intervened in his favor. Everything seemed to be a sign. In 1948, the great actress Elvire Popesco fell under the charm of the twenty-six-year-old creator. She was fifty-four at the time. Impressed, she invited him to Maxim's, a temple of French gastronomy. The menu boasted unlimited caviar and champagne. For her, a theater diva, this was normal. She was amazed to hear her guest proclaim, "Of course it's good. But nothing beats a good old-fashioned omelet, a little runny." She was even more amazed when, in 1981, the young man, who had by then become a fashion mogul and astute businessman, bought the very same Maxim's himself, and drank to her health during an evening with the who's who of Parisian society.

It was 1950 and a new chapter was beginning. Pierre was getting closer to his dream of beauty and fashion. Dior had enjoyed the support of Marcel Boussac, but Pierre, ever-thrifty, had only two million francs as they were at the time — or twenty thousand "new francs" as they would become when the system changed in 1960. With the help of Marcel Escoffier, he bought the Maison Pascaud, which specialized in theater costumes. He moved into a modest home high up on the fifth floor of 10 Rue Richepanse, on the edge of the eighth arrondissement. It was an attic loft of around 2,000 square feet—and due to become his atelier. He was twenty-eight years old and unstoppable. On the day of opening, in a heartfelt gesture, Dior sent him a beautiful bouquet of 144 roses.

High up in his perch, Pierre and his four employees set up shop with no outside help, forming a sort of "fashion commando." There was rent to pay, not to mention salaries and various other expenses. He had to bring in money, and had a trick up his sleeve: the world of theater and cinema. At Paquin and Dior, he had met the likes of Christian Jacques, Joseph Losey, Max Ophüls and Luchino Visconti, among others. He now went on to create costumes for ballets and actors, rubbing

Pierre Cardin posing on the steps of his private townhouse at 118 Rue du Faubourg Saint-Honoré, where he set up his fashion house in 1954. Photograph by Mark Shaw.

Making Fashion Modern

shoulders with Elvire Popesco, Gérard Philippe, Vivien Leigh and Rita Hayworth. His appetite was insatiable. He always wanted more, mobilized his contacts in the costume world, and took advantage of the Pascaud name to pivot to haute couture at the age of thirty. What a challenge! The war with its deficits and rationing was fading into the backdrop, and women were expecting more from those who dressed and accessorized them. Pierre didn't miss the boat, working tirelessly day and night to dress the highest-spending haute couture clients. He made the trousseau of the future Contesse de la Poype and that of a good number of her friends from English high society. Dior also sent him clients and even entrusted him with the making of certain costumes for balls, such as the *Bal des Rois et des Reines*, thrown by Étienne de Beaumont, and the *Bal du Siècle* that took place on September 3, 1951, at the Palazzo Labia in Venice, hosted by Charles de Beistegui. Pierre made the famous costumes of the white giants with huge black tricorn hats as conceived by Salvador Dalí.

Above:
One of the models presented in the 1957 collection—a cocktail coat in embossed silk.

Facing page:
Pierre Cardin next to a dressmaker's dummy. Thanks to his thorough training, the couturier knew all aspects of his trade: designing, drawing, cutting, testing, and sewing.

Facing page:
After successive stints at Paquin, Schiaparelli, and Dior, Pierre Cardin bought the Pascaud fashion house that specialized in stage costumes and launched his career as a couturier. Thanks to his extensive contacts, he worked for the theater and the cinema, and also helped create costumes for the most famous post-war balls, such as the winter ball at the Palais des Glaces in Paris, on December 7, 1954, to benefit underprivileged children.

Above and right:
In their costumes designed by Pierre Cardin for the winter ball in 1954, Patricia López Willshaw as a swan and Baron de Redé as Louis II of Bavaria. Photographs by André Ostier.

Pages 50–51:
Doris Brynner and Pierre Cardin at the winter ball at the Hotel de Coulanges, Place des Vosges, December 3, 1958.

Making Fashion Modern

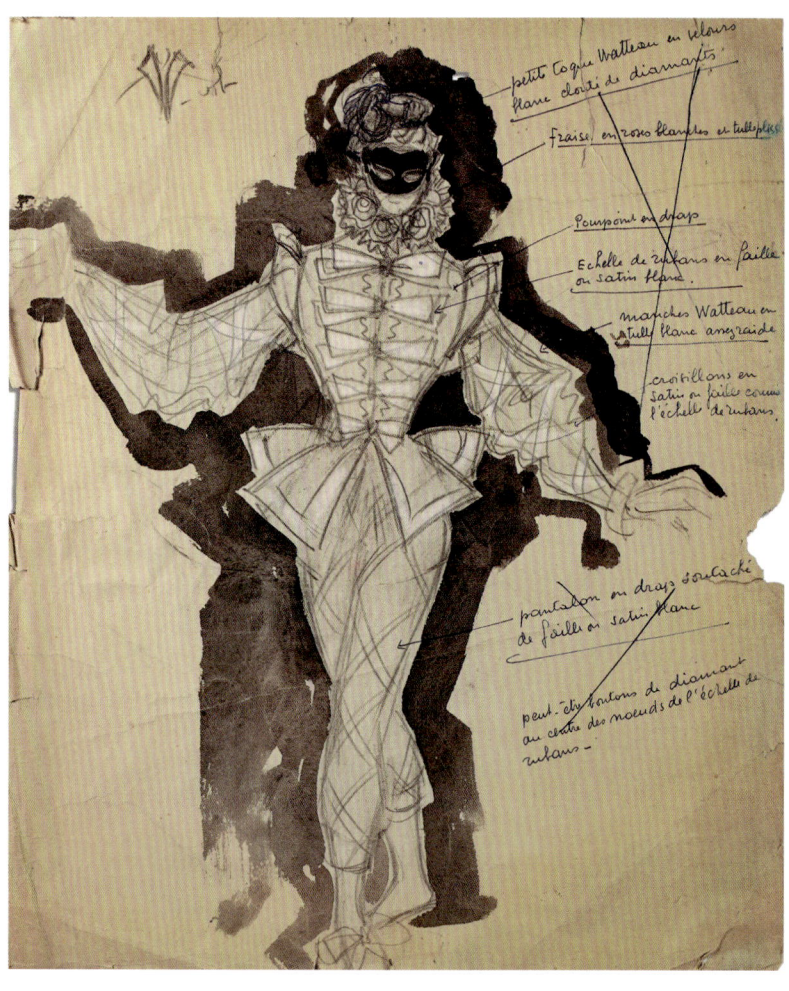

Three costume designs for the "Ball of the Century" given by Charles de Beistegui on September 3, 1951, at the Palazzo Labia in Venice.

Above:
An annotated watercolor of a harlequin costume made for the Duchess of Brissac.

Left:
A watercolor of a harlequin costume made for the Prince of Arenberg.

Facing page:
Study of a costume for the Beistegui ball, 1951. Christian Dior helped Pierre Cardin set up this costume workshop and sent him orders that he himself could not fulfil.

CONSTRUCTIONS AND CUTS, FIRST COLLECTIONS

In 1971, as a guest on a program on France Culture, Pierre Cardin reminded the world that his training as a couturier was particularly thorough: "I know how to draw, I know how to cut, I know how to do fittings, I know how to make a garment, I even know how to sew it. I think I have explored every aspect of my field, which is quite rare in this profession because most designers do not know how to sew. I really wanted to learn a trade from A to Z."

It is this mastery of all the stages of the design and manufacture of a garment that gave Pierre Cardin exceptional technical know-how and unequalled skill from the start. A brilliant tailor and cutter, Pierre gained fame after leaving Dior thanks to the success of his coats and jackets with structured cuts and clean lines, offering great freedom of movement. His first collections continued his research into proportions and volumes, influenced by his taste for architecture, geometry and asymmetry. Later, the fashion designer/artist defined his creations as living sculptures.

The first design in Pierre Cardin's first haute couture collection, Spring–Summer 1953. In this photograph taken by Philippe Pottier at Place Beauvau in Paris, the model Marie-Thérèse is wearing a wool gabardine.

Facing page:
Red wool pleated coat, 1953. This famous design, which sold thousands of models in the United States, marked the beginning of Pierre Cardin's fortune.

Above:
Pleated silk coat, 1953. The design was presented in an outdoor setting: the colonnade of the Musée d'art moderne in Paris.

Making Fashion Modern

Money was flowing in and it made sense to ride the wave. For Pierre, nothing less than being the best would do. For this reason, he decided that he would not be an actor or dancer. He thought about it time and time again but his beginnings in fashion had already met with success, offering a path to future glory.

A financially astute man, one rule guided his course: no bank loans and no debts. Only the money earned from his successful ventures in fashion was viable, though he did receive help in his early days from Arturo López Willshaw via an introduction by Alexis de Redé.

For his first collection, Pierre presented fifty looks and was bent on making a splash. Above all, he was drawn to one particular fabric—perhaps the lingering memory of the small white coat from his childhood? The fabric was called "Montagnac" and the designer wanted to use it to make a coat—a pleated one! He contacted an artisan who declared the idea impossible but the designer insisted, many tests were run, and lo and behold, it worked! Thanks to an excellent sales network and the tailor Oppenheimer, Pierre Cardin would sell no fewer than two hundred thousand of these innovative coats in the United States. It helped establish his name and gain traction.

At that time, America was the market leader in fashion, the one that called the shots and established the mood. In short, the ultimate trend-setter. Here again, Pierre's people skills and savoir faire for public relations worked wonders. Divas from the press and fashion world such as Carmel Snow *(Harper's Bazaar)*, Hélène Lazareff (Pierre Lazareff's wife, founder and director of *Elle* magazine), and Marie-Louise Bousquet (editor-in-chief of *Harper's Bazaar* in Paris) went so far as to venture up to his attic studio to lavish him with praise, joking that they had to take the freight elevator to get up there. In Pierre's attic, there were no chairs to speak of, much less armchairs. These fancy folks had to settle for a lowly stool. Pierre cleverly turned this to his advantage, providing a welcome contrast to Dior, a house that received guests in ostentatious salons decked out with expensive floral arrangements. He was young and could get away with anything. The women sang the praises of this incredibly gifted and handsome man; they wore his name with pride, sealing his reputation. From then on, Pierre knew how much he owed them—especially Hélène Lazareff who, completely won over by the designer, was his most loyal supporter. (At that time, all the great couturiers and designers were markedly older than Pierre—with one exception: Hubert de Givenchy, five years his junior.)

The media was abuzz. Thanks to his pleated coat, Pierre was the talk of the town. A bit surprised by this sudden rise to the top, he tried to stay true to himself and let his personality shine through. Nonetheless, at the tender age of thirty, he was already dressing the Begum (Yvonne Labrousse, the Aga Khan's wife), Lady Raine Spencer, Eva Perón and the Duchess of Westminster, to name just a few: all beacons of youth and icons around the world! Such a tremendous opportunity would not be lost on Pierre.

Throughout his life, style was his guiding principle. All creation is a leap into the future, and Pierre was hot on the heels of success. To his mind, two artist-designers were at the summit of the fashion world: Dior and Cristóbal Balenciaga. Perhaps for fear of not measuring up, he looked for his own route, searched for novelty and

The model Simone d'Aillencourt in a ratiné wool coat with an accordion pleated back, corolla collar, and "mushroom" hat. Photographed by Georges Dambier for *Elle*, 1958.

Above:
Suit with short jacket
and belted waist,
felt cloche hat, 1954.

Facing page:
Grey mottled wool
pencil suit with boatneck.
Photograph by
Mark Shaw taken in
the Tuileries Gardens
for *Life* magazine,
September 1957.

"Pierre Cardin is, in my opinion, the only young couturier who has the engineering genius required by the industry today, together with the imagination and taste that goes with the great dressmaking tradition of the past."

Charles James on Pierre Cardin, Women's Wear Daily, *July 5, 1956.*

Double-breasted slim-fit suit with scarf collar worn with a fur hat, 1953. A pure expression of the elegance of the Cardin style.

recognition, a double springboard. In 1954, he launched the "bubble dress." It all started with his observations of the versatility of muslin. Until then, this material had been the calling card of Madame Grès, who reigned over couture in Paris from 1935 to 1984. Pierre wanted to try his own hand at it. To do so, he created a balloon of muslin, "inflated" it by inserting a light fabric into it, and realized poetic dresses with an ethereal quality. Dresses so beautiful and so precious that it seemed they should only be worn once and then put away forever. Dresses as elusive as a mirage. In Vichy, Pierre had befriended Lucien Lamorisse, a student at the time, and now a talented and original filmmaker. He was working on his masterpiece *Le Ballon rouge* (*The Red Balloon*, 1956), which gave Pierre the idea of making muslin "balloons." Following the bubble dresses came balloon dresses in pastel shades of blue, yellow, green, and purple: swelling forms echoed by a very light lining. Pierre would often call them "dream dresses."

For Pierre, fashion was an art form — something that could capture the very soul of a civilization. He thought of himself, meanwhile, as an independent man, a kind of adventurer. In these years, he built himself up, equipped himself, and brought together men and women who would support him, such as the Baroness of Avilliers, former director of Lucien Lelong. Journalists liked him; he knew how to talk to them and win them over. He rose to the level of a "fashion founder," like Charles F. Worth, who had become, through talent and hard work, the official couturier of the Second Empire. On a more personal note, in 1952, Cardin's life was enriched by a new life-and-work partner, André Oliver. Originally from Toulouse, Oliver had come to Paris at the age of twenty to present his sketches to the young designer, who hired him on the spot. He quickly became his right-hand man and companion. He was an incredible master of fashion and elegance: Pierre's best ambassador! His dinner parties in his apartment on Rue du Cherche-Midi were among the most popular in Paris. For more than forty years, the two men were inseparable, mutually enriching each other as they advanced to the top. Pierre would often say of Oliver: "I have met my creative match!"

The famous "bubble dress" worn by Diane de Obaldia in the couture salons of Pierre Cardin, in 1954. Photograph by Roland de Vassal.

Pierre Cardin
in the fitting room
at 118 Rue du Faubourg
Saint-Honoré, on the eve
of a show, with his models
wearing percale patterns.
Photograph by
Roland de Vassal, 1958.

"One must always consider the whole silhouette, from the hat down to the shoes. When a new fashion is born, everything—hats, shoes, bags—must change shape to complement it. That is why I have found it necessary to design accessories as well as dresses. A costume is like a painting in which the separate elements unite to form a perfect whole."

Pierre Cardin, "Mr. Cardin Tells How to Be Chic," Chicago Daily Tribune, *November 24, 1958.*

Posing in the courtyard of 118 Rue du Faubourg Saint-Honoré, a model presents an evening coat in satin-weave silk, 1955.

Left:
Model Marie-Hélène Arnaud in a wool houndstooth blouson-style suit on the terrace of the future Publicis Drugstore overlooking the Place de l'Étoile and the Arc de Triomphe. Photograph by Georges Dambier for *Elle*, 1958.

Facing page:
Marie-Hélène Arnaud in a city suit trimmed with coarse satin. Photographed by Georges Dambier on Quai de la Mégisserie, Paris, 1957.

Page 72:
A wool suit consisting of a short jacket over a draped skirt, Fall–Winter collection 1957–58.

Page 73:
Model Hélène Delrieu in a houndstooth suit with a scoop-neck jacket. Contact sheet by Roland de Vassal, 1957.

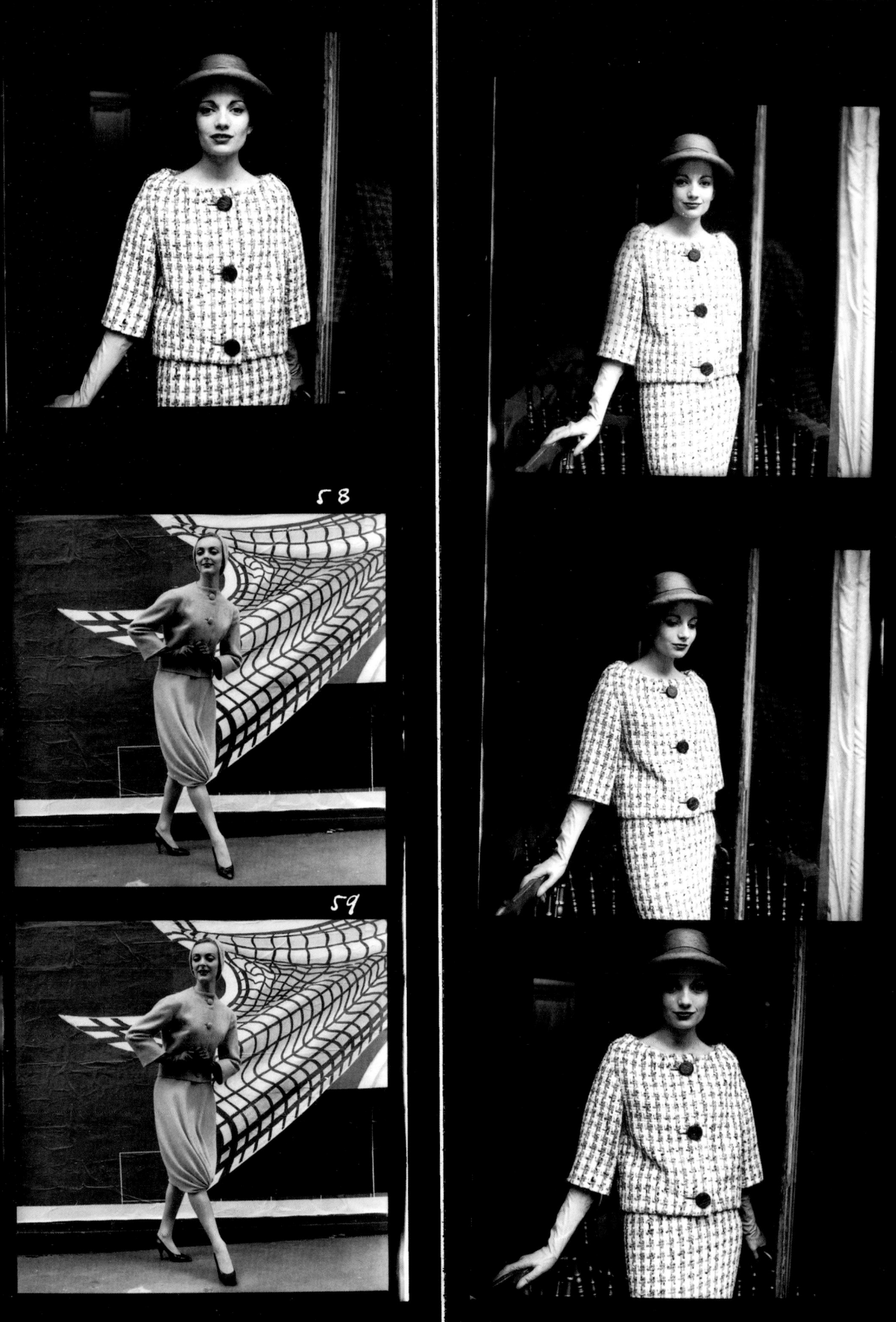

Facing page:
The soft lines of a wool coat draped down the back. Photograph by Roland de Vassal, 1958.

Above:
The model Bettina Graziani, known as Bettina, poses in a car in a coat with a corolla collar. Photograph by Georges Dambier.

Making Fashion Modern

Model Nena von Schlebrügge, mother of actress Uma Thurman, flying over the Seine and the Eiffel Tower in a helicopter, wearing a velvet hat by Pierre Cardin. Photograph by Norman Parkinson for *Queen* magazine, August 1960.

118 RUE DU FAUBOURG SAINT-HONORÉ

Pierre continued his path to success, leaving Rue Richepanse and moving with his team to 118 Rue du Faubourg Saint-Honoré, a hôtel particulier that belonged to the Harcourt family. One year later, he passed another threshold by opening a boutique for women on the second floor. The name on the sign was archetypal: that of *the* original woman, Eve. The company was put in good working order.

To evolve in the fashion world, one must do three things: create, manufacture, and sell. Pierre admitted his own ambition and did not hide the fact that he coveted success. He knew that PR was key. Accordingly, one day in 1954, a young Japanese press photographer came to take a series of pictures for various magazines from his homeland. Roland de Vassal, the in-house photographer, had suffered a minor injury. Pierre Cardin lost no time in asking the young Japanese woman to sub for him. No sooner said than done—and thus began a long and fruitful relationship.

Yoshi Takata became part of the "Cardin galaxy." She spent the rest of her life around Pierre, taking care of his PR, his business, his creations, and most importantly his image. A company with such stature needed many talents on many levels.

Some might have left it at that: haute couture. But Pierre Cardin was a visionary. Dressing women is one thing…but what about men? Was there anything to be done there? Sexist and gendered thinking was still rampant at the time. Men's wardrobes were limited to the dull palette of the nineteenth-century bourgeoisie: black, gray, brown and navy blue. The only whims a self-respecting man could permit himself were ties, jacket linings, slippers, and dressing gowns. Pierre treaded lightly therefore, starting with ties and shirts. Yet once again, he made some daring moves, creating ties and shirts with floral motifs. In a world where a simple blue end-on-end shirt, with its contrasting warp and weft, made people talk, this was nothing short of a revolution! But Pierre Cardin was fearless, infusing color and fun into an otherwise drab and strict universe. Another of his guiding principles: never let up.

If Eve catered to a female clientele, Adam would be its masculine counterpart. It was 1957 and here it was, Pierre's second boutique. One could be forgiven for thinking that Pierre was simply selling accessories for men—but of course, this

Pierre Cardin photographed around 1955 in front of 118 Rue du Faubourg Saint-Honoré, the former mansion of the Harcourt family.

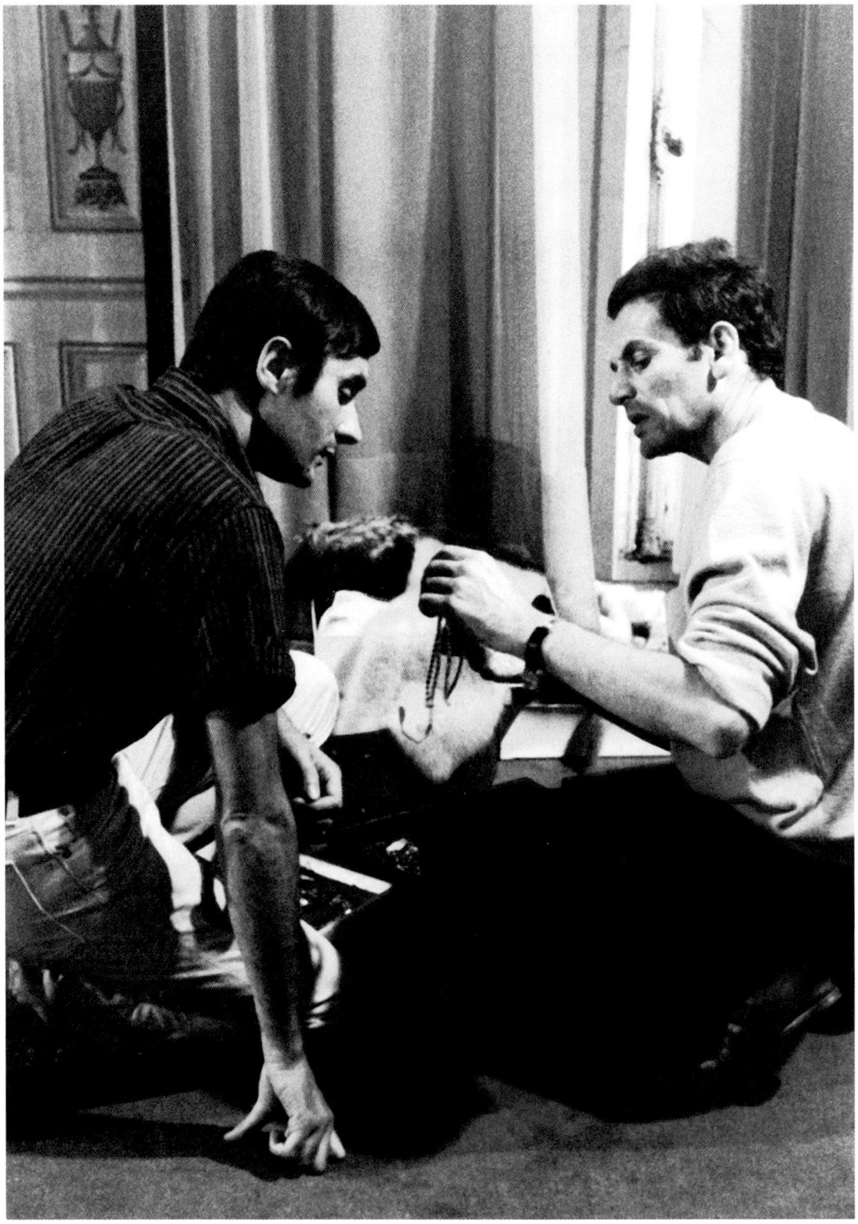

Above:
André Oliver and Pierre Cardin. Oliver worked with the designer for over forty years and was his lifelong companion.

Right:
Pierre Cardin in his workshop at 118 Rue du Faubourg Saint-Honoré, selecting fabrics.

was a mere step towards his real goal: a complete range of men's ready-to-wear clothing. In no time, a line of suits was launched.

In the nineteenth century, Great Britain and Italy were the shop windows of fashion in Europe, relegating France to a minor role. Pierre saw in this an opportunity. He may have been a beginner, but he knew that he could tap into his strong ties to actors, musicians, writers, and film directors. Afterall, why couldn't they play the role of clients? They liked being in the spotlight and were happy to be Pierre's walking billboards.

Pierre Cardin in front of the window of his boutique at 118 Rue du Faubourg Saint-Honoré, looking at the display of accessories. The designer's innate elegance would come to revolutionize men's fashion.

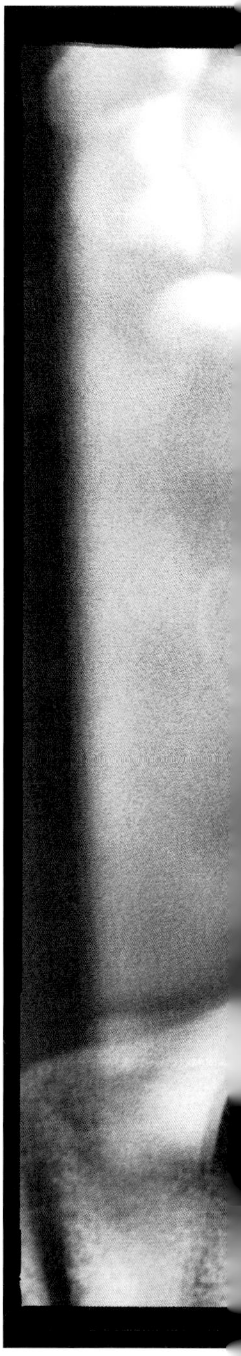

Left:
Aware of the growing importance of the media, Cardin began to shape his image in the 1960s, playing on his multiple statuses as designer, entrepreneur, and businessman.

Above:
For the designer,
"Creation is a personal
silhouette, the abstraction
of an image I have in mind
that I try to impose first
through a drawing, then
by a cut, and finally into
a garment."

Above and facing page: Marie-Hélène Arnaud at Place de la Concorde in a wool coat with a funnel collar. Photographs by Georges Dambier for *Elle*, March 4, 1957.

Pages 88–89: A series of photographs by Roland de Vassal in 1957, in which a Citroën DS, the mythical car of the time, serves as a backdrop for a model wearing a silk crepe cocktail dress belted at the waist. Some fifty years later, Pierre Cardin tried to recreate the design— one of his favorites— from a photograph, but admitted he was unable to.

Facing page:
Actress Karen
Blanguernon wears
a thick wool double-
breasted and belted coat
with a Claudine collar
and raglan sleeves.
Photograph by
Georges Dambier
for *Elle*, March 11, 1960.

Above:
Karen Blanguernon
in a wool gabardine
coat with flared collar.
Photograph by
Georges Dambier, 1960.

Facing page:
A tweed cocktail suit, three-quarter length sleeves and cape collar, 1958.

Above:
A detail of the same suit kept in the Cardin archives.

Page 94:
A woolen crepe coat dress with tied martingale on the front. Photograph by Willy Maywald at the Saint-Ouen flea market, 1954.

Page 95:
Anna Karina was a model for Cardin before making her film debut with Jean-Luc Godard. Here, she is wearing a double-breasted coat in wool gabardine with three-quarter length sleeves that show off her long gloves. Photograph by Georges Dambier, 1958.

A WORLD OF INSPIRATION

Pierre was advancing on several fronts: not only was he breaking sartorial codes, he was also re-drawing the map of the world around him. Despite the seemingly permanent East-West divide, Pierre felt that this too was destined to change. The USSR and the East would surely open to consumerism sooner or later. He was getting a glimpse of new worlds to come. He packed up the tools of his trade and set out for Japan, the USSR, and China, acting as a sort of cultural and artistic ambassador. The couturier flew to the United States in 1957, and then to a Japan in the midst of full-blown cultural and industrial revolution (on route he became one of the first to fly the new Air France Paris-Tokyo route, which passed through Anchorage, Alaska).

Post-war Japan was a distant and closed land. In the eighteenth century, religious pilgrims from the West were very badly perceived by the locals, which had considerably hindered trade with Europe. The Meiji era, which started during the second part of the nineteenth century, led to a new opening onto the world. But wartime defeat against the British and Americans, not to mention the devastation of two atomic bombs, had shaken Japan to its core. To restore diplomacy and trade, it was necessary to start all over again. Fortunately, the Cardini family originated from Veneto, the interface between West and East—and all Venetians, besides, feel like descendants of the bold Marco Polo.

Soon, air transport blossomed: Air France's new Paris-Anchorage-Tokyo route used Lockheed Super Star liners—airplanes with propellers. The flight took no less than thirty hours. For Pierre, Japan was a far-flung place. The only thing he knew of it was the Japanese Embassy in Paris and Yoshi Takata, who was to be his guide. Through her, he worked for the Japanese Design Federation, teaching pattern-cutting and presenting collections. He taught daily classes at the Bunka Fukuso fashion institute and designer Chiyo Tanaka's fashion college. East and West were still worlds apart. Globalization had not yet done its job of polishing and standardizing everything. Japan remained an island, where people still clung to distinctive identities; clothes, customs, language, and food were all strongly codified there. But in Pierre's case, universal talent trumped nationality. His life in Japan was very pleasant and he forged strong ties with the local culture.

While in the country, he felt at home at the Bunka Fukuso school, where he taught three-dimensional cutting for a month as an honorary professor. This world-renowned school, an icon of Japan's industrial success, offered training in design,

From a very young age, Pierre Cardin wanted to travel the world. He did so throughout his life to expand his fashion empire to China, Russia, Japan, and Australia.

Left:
Pierre Cardin posing
on the Giza plateau
in front of the pyramids
during his first fashion
show in Egypt, c. 1955.

Above:
The models accompanying
the designer wear
taffeta cocktail dresses,
the second on the left
in guipure lace.

technology, marketing, and fashion. Pierre was not yet forty years old but he was well on his way to greatness.

With typical foresight, Pierre had come accompanied by a western model, Hélène. But once on the ground, he also hired Japanese models to bring his works to life. He pre-selected some two hundred young women, one of whom completely enchanted him: Hiroko Matsumoto. She became his muse and he wanted to bring her back to Paris. It would take him three years to convince her.

Hiroko arrived in Paris on a Sunday in 1960, a real Japanese doll, aged only twenty. The employee from Maison Cardin in charge of picking her up and getting her settled in Paris forgot all about her. Stranded at Orly airport, she sat down and began to cry. A sorry opening but the rest is the stuff of movies: Pierre would make her a top model, a huge success. He launched her on the Parisian scene, inaugurating the era of young women come from other horizons to breathe life into dazzling garments, if only for the time of a fashion show. This was a real achievement at the time. Proud of his muse, the designer had her wear the wedding dress, which traditionally closed haute couture presentations, fourteen times over seven years of close collaboration. When Hiroko got pregnant this chapter ended and a new phase of her life began.

Meanwhile, in Japan, the Cardin brand was now well-established. In his honor, the Pierre Cardin Prize was created, awarded to the best designer of the year at the Bunka Fashion College.

Left:
Pierre Cardin leafing through *Women's Wear Daily*, whose editor, John Fairchild, was a close friend. To have an article dedicated to him in this widely read journal in the fashion world was a great honor for the couturier.

Facing page:
Pierre Cardin in New York posing on the Rockefeller Center terrace in front of the Empire State Building. The designer was fascinated by the vitality of this city.

In the 1960s, Pierre felt that haute couture was stagnating, and he began to diversify. He opened ready-to-wear outlets at several department stores: Printemps in Paris, Rinascente in Milan, Selfridges in London, Herty in Germany, and Takashimaya in Tokyo. The licensing contracts began to pile up. Fashion was becoming more democratic.

Now others were starting to come to him instead of the other way around. He was enjoying real recognition. As he said in a long interview with the French monthly magazine the *Revue des Deux Mondes*, in January 1993: "I am a happy Sisyphus!" He oversaw everything, supervised everything, and on a daily basis signed three hundred checks, copying the sales figures of his activities, by hand, into small notebooks. He was steering a kind of ocean liner, a whole world unto itself.

By now Pierre had deep pockets. He was reaping the fruits of his creativity and vision, he was on a roll. He could afford to invent fresh and new things and to shake the old things up a bit. Two words best define his creations and collections: innovation and elegance. The "Cardin style" was easily recognizable, and he took it in several directions. The shapes of his works started to become sculptural, featuring draping, curves, and geometric forms. As he used to say at the time, women would fill these receptacles of fabric and creativity with their own bodies. For Pierre Cardin, elegance was a masterclass—no less.

Pierre always maintained a pronounced taste for purity of line. According to him, simplicity was the only thing he truly liked. By his own admittance, he harbored a desire to dress not only the Duchess of Windsor but also her concierge. In the case of the duchess, he pulled it off: she came to be dressed by him, and then came back with close friends, all eager to wear Pierre Cardin. Pierre was an artist blazing a trail of his own making, eager to suck out all the marrow of life.

Pierre Cardin on his first trip to Japan in 1957, photographed by his friend and collaborator Yoshi Takata in front of the great Buddha of the Kotoku-in temple in Kamakura.

At the request of the
Japanese Design
Federation, Pierre Cardin
taught cutting and
presented his collections
at the Bunka Fukuso
and Tanaka Chiyo
fashion schools.

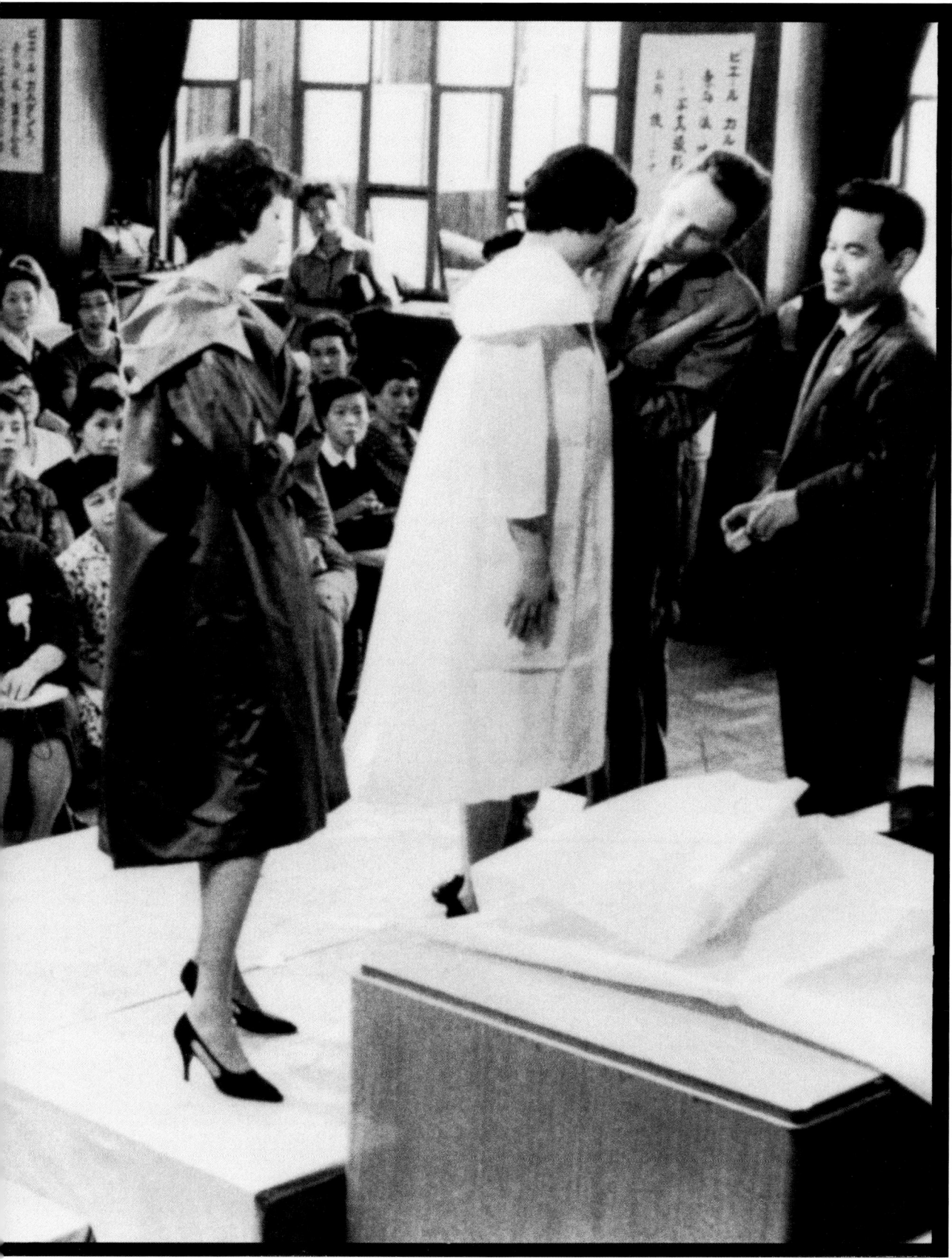

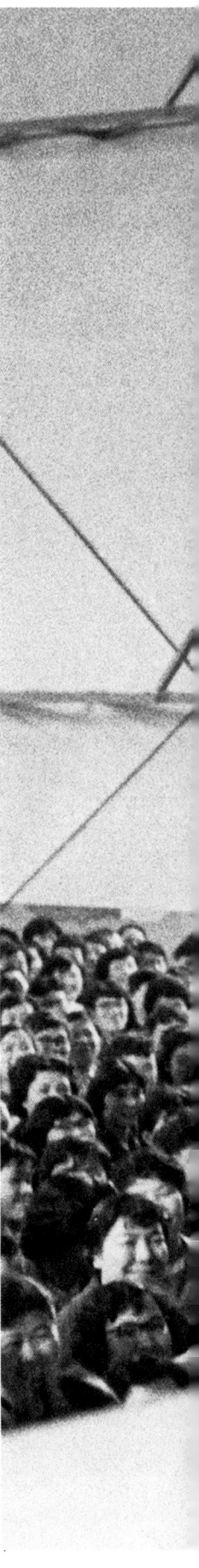

Above:
Yoshi Takata was Pierre Cardin's guide in his discovery of Japanese culture. A theater enthusiast, the designer was curious about the art of kabuki and the meticulous preparation of the actors' sophisticated make-up and costumes.

Facing page:
Pierre Cardin at Bunka Fukuso's school of dressmaking and styling, where he taught three-dimensional cutting for a month as an honorary professor.

HIROKO MATSUMOTO
Pierre Cardin met Hiroko Matsumoto in 1957 during his first trip to Japan. Already a renowned model in her own country, Matsumoto hesitated for three years before finally agreeing to follow the designer to Paris, where she became his muse. Her grace, purity, and fragility fascinated Cardin who made her his preferred model, propelling the twenty-year-old to the summit of the fashion world. With a fringed-bob cut, imperturbable and mysterious face, and graceful silhouette that seemed to float, Hiroko's style was all the rage and made her the first famous Japanese model in the West. *Vogue*, *Harper's Baazar*, and *Elle* all rushed to do shoots with her and the greatest photographers, from Avedon to Newton, sought her out. She was an icon. So much so that François Truffaut, champion of the New Wave of French cinema, chose her to play Kyoko, Antoine Doinel/Jean-Pierre Léaud's mistress in *Domicile Conjugal* in 1970. The credits list her as Mademoiselle Hiroko. In 1967 she married Henri Berghauer, director of Pierre Cardin boutiques, and set sail for other horizons.

Facing page:
Pierre Cardin in the middle of a design session for a checkered wool garment with Hiroko, his favorite Japanese model.

Page 110:
In the courtyard of the private mansion at 118 Rue du Faubourg Saint-Honoré, Hiroko wearing an evening gown with a silk duchesse satin skirt in the early 1960s.

Page 111:
Hiroko in the haute couture salon at 118 Rue du Faubourg Saint-Honoré in a so-called "tube" evening gown with multicolored sequin embroidery, 1964.

Page 112:
Hiroko fittings photographed by Roland de Vassal.

Page 113:
Wool crepe cocktail dress and coat with holes, suede belt and sable neckline, 1965.

Left:
Hiroko on the quays of the Seine photographed in August 1969 by Pierluigi Praturlon. She is wearing the first trapeze dress in jersey, Spring–Summer 1968 collection.

"I only like creation and I like to see it worn, consequently I always desired to see my pieces in the street. Only having them in a couture salon doesn't interest me in the slightest, seeing them on hangers, to say "I've made something new that I don't see in the street," gives me no satisfaction. I like to create and I like what I've made to sell, that is my joy."

Pierre Cardin, Paradoxes, *France Culture, Radio France, INA, 1971.*

André Oliver
in Pierre Cardin's living
room with two models,
Françoise and Mome,
in sequin embroidered
evening dresses.

THE CARDIN UNIVERSE

As early as 1957, Pierre was drawing lessons from the practices of Christian Dior, who had built the foundations of a veritable empire with astonishing speed. To get around customs duties, he set up partnerships with companies that manufactured Dior-branded products. He institutionalized a system by opening public relations offices around the world. In the same way, Pierre signed a licensing agreement with a clothing manufacturer in Lyon. The first year was a flop; it was difficult to innovate on unstable ground. The couturier-entrepreneur took a step back, reflected and changed tack. A new contract in 1959 met with success, with both parties eager to move forward. Consequently, Pierre branched out and developed licenses in many countries.

Just as the second half of the nineteenth century brought novelties like standardized sizing for clothes and exchanges in the event of buyer's remorse, Pierre was set to conquer a new sector: ready-to-wear, a fashion revolution! Ever the pioneer, he took fashion to the streets. The haute couture trade union reacted violently, lashing out at Pierre by sending him into long-term exile. He wasn't having it. How dare they ban him? There was only one thing to do. He responded by branching out into more sectors: perfume, furniture, sheets, household linens, luggage. He was shaking up the codes of a closed world and it was working! Very effective PR left the couture snobs in the dust, resentful of his sphere of influence.

1959 was a real turning point in the designer's career. Ever the iconoclast, he boldly presented his first women's ready-to-wear collection at Printemps, on Boulevard Haussmann. Until then, Pierre had flirted with the heights, but one thing still bothered him: only the wealthy could afford to shop in couture houses—haute couture being the preserve of just a handful of rich people. Why not open a department-store-style operation, allowing as many as possible to enjoy beautifully made clothes at an affordable price? Even those who aren't rich deserve to dress elegantly. Moreover, Pierre suspected that in the West, the elites would soon dissolve; the overprotected world of high society, which spent lavishly, would disappear. In addition, people were starting to travel much more. Under such conditions, the cocktail dress would have to give way to so-called sportswear—it was simply inevitable.

The world of haute couture looked on with worry. What to make of a man, known for his refinement, who was breaking all the usual rules by democratizing this "aristocratic" fiefdom? For those who belonged to the old order, it was nothing less than suicide.

Pierre Cardin, Guy Laroche, and Yves Saint Laurent on the cover of *Elle* in the spring of 1958. "These three young men have rejuvenated fashion," reads the headline. The 36-year-old Cardin was the head of a house of 170 workers and 6 models.

Angelica Lazansky von Bukowa, the future Lady Cawdor, modeled for Pierre Cardin in his early days. Here during the representation of *Norma*, with Maria Callas, in May 1964 at the Opéra de Paris.

The creator looked to the public for recognition. Ever attentive to a changing world, he tapped into youth and its insatiable desires, becoming the leading designer of the sixties with his colorful miniskirts and ultra-modern silhouettes. His name and image spread like wildfire.

Since he had two feet, he decided to straddle each branch of fashion: he put one foot in haute couture, which benefitted from the recognition of experts; and one in ready-to-wear, acclaimed by the general public. Since the Second Empire, ready-to-wear had developed considerably. The innovator was the Bon Marché department store, revamped in 1852, and later providing inspiration for Émile Zola's novel *Au Bonheur des Dames (The Ladies' Delight)*. The Belle Jardinière, Printemps, Samaritaine and Galeries Lafayette soon followed suit—all of which have left their mark on the city of Paris and its history.

Fashion moguls reproached Pierre for daring to present his first women's ready-to-wear collection at Printemps. It took a lot of nerve to rock the closed world of Parisian salons. Known for his elegance and refinement, Pierre thumbed his nose at tradition by knocking down the walls of a highly private domain. Bringing his creations within reach of the average citizen, he allowed the public to finally see what only a happy few could enjoy. He forewent the magnificent armchairs installed in sumptuous salons and hired less sophisticated models. The presentation was a great hit, the punishment paradoxical: Pierre was forced to resign for having upset the rules of the haute couture trade association. But he didn't care.

For him, it was simple: high fashion and ready-to-wear were two sides of the same coin—mutually supportive. What's more, he found it amusing to be lambasted by the establishment at the same moment as he was delightedly witnessing his counterparts all lining up to do ready-to-wear. There was ranting and raving, but Pierre knew what he was doing. He may have taken a hit in the couture and creativity department, but he was lining his pockets with his ready-to-wear earnings. Each helped the other, and this was undoubtedly the way to go.

The wolves were baying on all sides: "Monsieur Cardin, in two years, nobody will be talking about you anymore! You will fall into vulgarity, into the easy way out, it will be the end of the House of Cardin!" Very insightful!

In fact, the fashion world could not have been more mistaken. There were no fewer than three Golden Thimbles, the prestigious French fashion award, in Pierre's future. Fashion was propelled forward thanks to his rich and sumptuous creations, the master designer saturating a new market. Pierre met with tremendous success in women's fashion. He was becoming a household name; there was a whole other audience to seduce.

Starting in the nineteenth century, the New World had become a prerequisite for those who sought power. At first, Europeans invested in it, exploited it, idealized it. Interest in the New World grew after the Great War as Europe slowly started to decline and America began to shine. Pierre, always scouting the horizon, realized how important it was to follow in the footsteps of Christopher Columbus and Jacques Cartier. The future now lay westward. In the nineteenth century, after Stendhal, people used to say, "Here I come, Paris!" In the twentieth, they said— as Cardin himself would—"Here I come, America!" He understood that the United States had been a heavyweight since the end of the Second World War, in terms of both status and size; it offered a kaleidoscope of images, and promoted

A reception at Pierre Cardin's house given in honor of Maria Callas after her performance of *Norma* in May 1964. In the Quai Anatole-France apartment, the diva appears alongside Bernard and Annabel Buffet, friends of the couturier. Photograph by Yoshi Takata.

Annabel and Bernard Buffet in front of Pierre Cardin's boutique after a fashion show on January 29, 1966. The couple, who were very prominent in Paris at the time, attended the designer's parties. Annabel Buffet, born Schwob de Lure, modeled for Cardin.

André Oliver's apartment on Rue du Cherche-Midi, with paintings by Bernard Buffet on the walls. André Oliver was close to the painter and godfather to his son. Pierre Cardin used this apartment for social dinners.

consumerist values and a culture of success—all of which enchanted him. He knew, however, that he needed an astute commercial go-between, someone high up and well-known who could open doors for him everywhere that fashion and luxury called home.

Charles de Gaulle's presidency was marked by difficult relations with the United States. Since 1956, the French ambassador to the US had been Hervé Alphand, who had come to blows with the officials of Vichy-era France. In 1958, he married Nicole Merenda who, in her guise as Director of Haute Couture at Cardin, was deemed one of the most elegant women in the world. The Alphands brought a dash of pizazz to the French Embassy. The "pillar" on which madame the ambassador's wife would come to rely was none other than Jacqueline Bouvier Kennedy—not least since the future wife of the American president had loved Pierre's "plissé soleil" coat from 1953. Nicole Alphand had tenuous links to the iconic American "first" couple. Yet the *Washington Post* (cited in *Le Monde*, October 21, 1965) would say: "The American friends of the embassy and of Mrs Alphand had to go back to the eighteenth century to find someone who, in their opinion, had done more for Franco-American friendship."

Thanks to Nicole Alphand's network, the world of American show biz would fall in love with Pierre Cardin and his wildly innovative creations. Lauren Bacall, nicknamed "The Look," was smitten with his work, as was her daughter, Leslie Bogart. And then there was Elizabeth Taylor, an absolute star, the statuesque Raquel Welch, and the American diva Dionne Warwick, who would pose in a Cardin gown on the cover of her album *Make Way for Dionne Warwick*, all the while applauding the couturier's choice to have "international" models walk the runway in the 1960s. "That diversity was refreshing," she said. Pierre started signing his first licensing contracts with American manufacturers. Upper-class Wasps developed a taste for the quality of his clothes and linens and were ready to follow him in his march towards luxury and beauty.

André Oliver joined Pierre Cardin in 1952. He was his right-hand man, life companion, and a faithful friend until his death in 1993. Photograph by Yoshi Takata.

Making Fashion Modern

"I like women of value, women with character. There is no arrivism in my choices. It's a choice by instinct. I like women who are out of the ordinary. Personality and class affect me more than a model or an actress."

Pierre Cardin, "Je suis un Sisyphe heureux," interview with Isabelle Dillmann de Jarnac, Revue des Deux Mondes, *January 1993.*

Brigitte Bardot in Scotland in 1966 on the set of the film *Two Weeks in September*, co-starring Laurent Terzieff. Pierre Cardin designed the actress's costumes, such as this wedding dress in organza and ostrich feathers.

Left:
Anouk Aimée at a fitting at 118 Faubourg Saint-Honoré in 1967. The actress is wearing a chiffon dress with flame-like embroidery.

Facing page:
Mia Farrow in an organza dress with flower incrustations in her husband Frank Sinatra's London apartment. Photographed in 1968 for *Life* and *Harper's Bazaar* by Bill Eppridge.

In 1966, Jacques Dutronc sang lyrics by Jacques Lanzmann that referenced the couturier: "There are professional playboys dressed by Cardin with shoes by Carvil." The singer is shown here at Place Beauvau, leaving Pierre Cardin's house with packages spilling out from his arms.

On the occasion of his first concert at the Olympia on June 1, 1967, Sammy Davis Jr. was photographed at a fitting in the Adam boutique at 59 Rue du Faubourg Saint-Honoré.

CARDIN AND THE WORLD OF PERFORMING ARTS

"I could've been an actor, or even a dancer. I took drama classes, but I was fearful of not being the best," declared Pierre Cardin. The designer would initially explore this fascination for the world of the performing arts by creating costumes for many plays and films and then, having established himself as a designer, by dressing all the celebrities of his era, from Brigitte Bardot to Elizabeth Taylor and Audrey Hepburn, as well as Mia Farrow, the Beatles, and Dionne Warwick. He worked with the greatest film and theater directors of the time: Christian Jacques, Jean Delannoy, Max Ophüls, and Luchino Visconti.

Above all, Cardin pursued his artistic passion through his namesake venue, the Espace Pierre Cardin, as the old Théâtre des Ambassadeurs was transformed into a temple of Parisian culture in the 1970s and 1980s. Avant-garde shows were held one after another, from the memorable performances of the *Prologue to Deafman Glance* by Bob Wilson in 1971, and *The Ride across Lake Constance* by Peter Handke in 1974, with Jeanne Moreau and Gérard Depardieu, to *The Madwoman of Chaillot*, with Maïa Plissetskaïa, in 1992. Not to mention exceptional concerts such as Marlene Dietrich's farewell performances in 1973, and Ella Fitzgerald's unforgettable recital in 1974.

On the cover of her 1964 album, *Make Way for Dionne Warwick*, the singer wore a dress by Pierre Cardin that she found, in her own words, "absolutely divine." She emphasized how the designer helped define modernity in the 1960s and opened up the fashion world to women of color like herself. To show her appreciation, she gave a recital at the Espace Cardin in November 1973.

Facing page:
Nicole Alphand in an evening gown. The wife of Hervé Alphand, French ambassador to the United States from 1956 to 1965, she was director of Maison Pierre Cardin from 1967, drawing a prestigious American clientele to the fashion house.

Top:
Jackie Kennedy with Nicole Alphand, after a visit to the Place Beauvau boutique, March 19, 1970.

Bottom:
Lee Radziwill in Cardin. The designer had formed close ties with the Bouvier sisters during a trip to Capri. Photograph by Yoshi Takata.

Facing page:
Jimmy Smith, Pierre Cardin's favorite model, modeling in 1966 in the salons of 118 Rue du Faubourg Saint-Honoré. In the front row, from left to right, the future President of the United States, Richard Nixon; his wife Patricia; Bernard Buffet, and Jacqueline Delubac. Photograph by Yoshi Takata.

Pages 144–45:
Photograph by Yoshi Takata of Countess Cristiana Brandolini d'Adda, sister of Gianni Agnelli, during an evening in André Oliver's salon. Countess Brandolini was Oliver's neighbor and a close friend of Pierre Cardin. The parties organized by the designer attracted the international jet set.

Making Fashion Modern

Facing page:
Pierre Cardin wearing indoor dress on the Quai Anatole-France in Paris, 1968. The designer agreed to pose at home for a CBS report on the launch of the Fall–Winter collections in Paris.

Above:
Lauren Bacall and Pierre Cardin in the Quai Anatole-France apartment. The American actress was the first to wear the famous "Cardine" dress, an iconic design by Pierre Cardin.

Pages 148–49:
An evening with friends at André Oliver's home, February 1970. From left to right: Françoise Hardy, André Oliver, Gilbert Bécaud, Annabel Buffet, Frédéric Botton, Pierre Cardin, and Bernard Buffet.

THE NEW STAR OF MEN'S FASHION

Pierre was cruising now and set out to conquer a new frontier: men's fashion. His objective was to bring a ray of light into this stuffy, closeted universe. Until then, men had been confined to geometric straightjackets when it came to clothing. Pierre wanted to see men—all men—in something softer, rounder, more form-fitting.

The 1960s brought significant lifestyle changes in the West. Consumption was on the rise, life quality was improving, and people had a desire for beauty and comfort. The time was ripe for Pierre to present his new collection for men. But, he wondered, should he go about parading young men in the salons of Rue du Faubourg Saint-Honoré? Two brilliant ideas came to him: rent the Hôtel de Crillon and hire two hundred young male students as models for the day. It's not hard to imagine the shock of university heads when a voice at the other end of the line said, "Hello, this is Pierre Cardin. Can you provide me with students to present my new collection? And others, too, to act as models? And still others to sit in the audience?" A cheeky and original request, to say the least. The students were gathered in the sumptuous Hôtel de Crillon, sixteen of them serving as "flag bearers" on the occasion—models for a day and, doubtless, the most handsome amongst them for other days too. As a reward for their work, they were offered a copious lunch alongside a fee. At first, they were bashful. Afterall, this was the 1960s and the students were little like the models of today. But bit by bit, things thawed, helped along by champagne, wine and whisky. The party was in full swing, and the press was out in force, from France and further afield. Pierre prudently hadn't invited the British media, of whom he was wary. The next day he was stunned to read laudatory articles in the French and American papers—but even more stunned by the title of an English publication: "The new star of men's fashion: Pierre Cardin." The Brits had come without his knowledge, which he took as quite the complement.

Pierre Cardin playing the model in a beaver coat in an Excalibur. Photograph by Lionel Kazan for an article in *Marie-Claire*, 1967, entitled "L'homme qui va plus vite que la mode" ("The man who moves faster than fashion").

The *New York Herald Tribune*, the *Daily Mail*, *Le Figaro*…all praised "the new creator of men's fashion." This was extraordinary press coverage that launched a dream career: that of Pierre Cardin, who would henceforth juggle haute couture, made-to-measure fashion, and ready-to-wear.

In terms of men's clothing—only of moderate interest to the world of "French couture"—Pierre sought to infuse his brand with a haute couture style.

The designer projected the image of a new kind of dandyism. Photos showed him sporting "casual" dress: grey flannel pants, without turn-ups, round-collared jackets and turtleneck sweaters. Within a few months, Pierre Cardin jackets, with or without round collars, and single-breasted, had become famous all over the world. Men now dreamed of being able to dress in Pierre Cardin.

The greatest honor came from the other side of the Channel: the Beatles placed an order for new stage suits in black and gray, without collars. The Beatles/Cardin "duet" toured the world, taking the designer's image and reach to new heights. He also created costumes for the actors of the British cult television series *The Avengers* (bowler hats and leather boots), not to mention the Rolling Stones, Sammy Davis Jr., Jacques Dutronc, Claude François, and Johnny Halliday. Another social group came knocking on Pierre's door: athletes, who were just beginning to polish their image and leave behind the world of "amateurism" that had previously held sway. Pierre had launched a revolution in men's clothing.

With variety music under his belt, the world of classical music came next. The Orchestra of Paris, conducted by Charles Munch, would perform all over the world dressed in suits designed by Pierre Cardin. Here again, a golden name and a golden touch proved a winning combination.

Pages 152–53:
Pierre Cardin was the first to use male models—chosen from 250 students—during the presentation of his first menswear collection at the Hôtel de Crillon, in 1958. Here, a photo session at the designer's home with photographer Yoshi Takata.

Facing page:
Jimmy Smith in a wool frock coat, strolling down Avenue Gabriel.

Pages 156–57:
Presentation of the menswear collection on September 27, 1963. Classic British style revisited by Pierre Cardin.

Page 158:
Waterproof checkered tweed coat with mock turtleneck.

Page 159:
Contact sheet by Roland de Vassal, photography series inspired by the designer's passion for traveling.

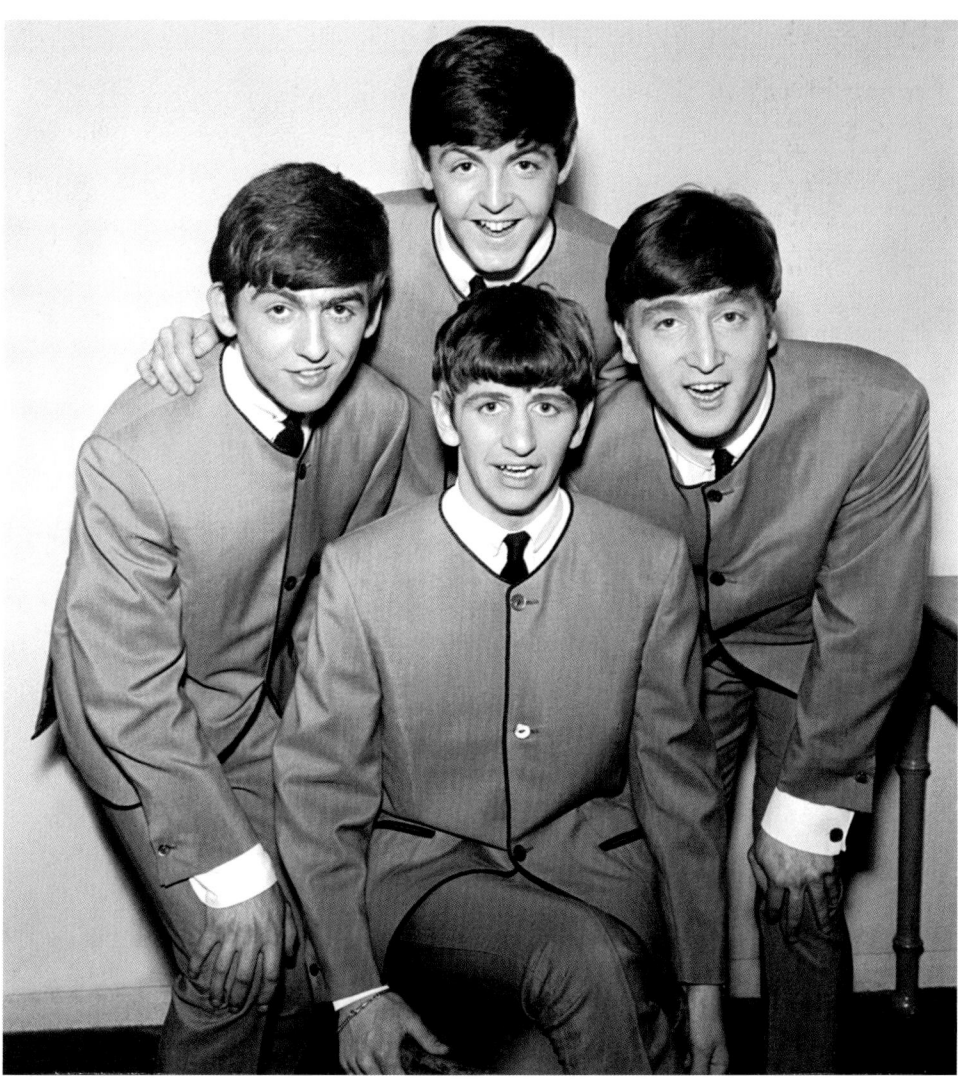

CARDIN AND THE BEATLES

At the insistence of their manager, Brian Epstein, the Beatles adopted suits devoid of collars and lapels in 1963, an adaptation of the jacket worn by Indian Prime Minister Nehru. When asked about this outfit with futuristic features, they exclaimed, "We got it from Paris, Pierre Cardin!" Inspired by his 1960 Cylinder collection, the designer's suit, "elegant and innovative, in light materials," has since become legendary in the world of rock 'n' roll. Later, the designer Douglas Millings made other versions of the same model, adopted as the band's signature suit. Many years later, and before creating her own fashion house, Paul McCartney's daughter Stella visited Cardin, whom she greatly admired.

Facing page:
Pierre Cardin by Roland de Vassal. A nod to *The Avengers* series in which the designer dressed the stars Patrick Macnee and Diana Rigg.

Above:
The Beatles in their famous suits designed by Cardin with no collars and no lapels. This photograph by Harry Hammond, taken during the band's first concert at the London Palladium in 1963, has gone down in history.

"We may live to see the day when husbands will say to their wives, 'What do you think of my new Cardin suit?'"

Pierre Cardin, "Cardin Designs Bright Plumage for the Males," New York Times, *March 15, 1960.*

Page 162:
Collarless linen suit from the Spring–Summer 1960 collection.

Page 163:
Double-breasted 7/8 length coat in Prince of Wales wool.

Facing page:
Pierre Cardin poses in a tartan golf trouser suit. Photograph by Roland de Vassal, March 1960.

Pages 166–67:
Daily Mirror journalist Christopher Ward wearing one of Pierre Cardin's revolutionary creations: a sleeveless space age tunic suit with rolled neck from the Cosmocorps collection. This photo shoot in the streets and airport of London in August 1966 captured a true cultural confrontation between tradition and modernity.

Above:
A hunting pea jacket worn with a riding hat.

Facing page:
In the main courtyard of the Invalides in Paris, dominated by the statue of Napoleon, two models in jackets, 1963.

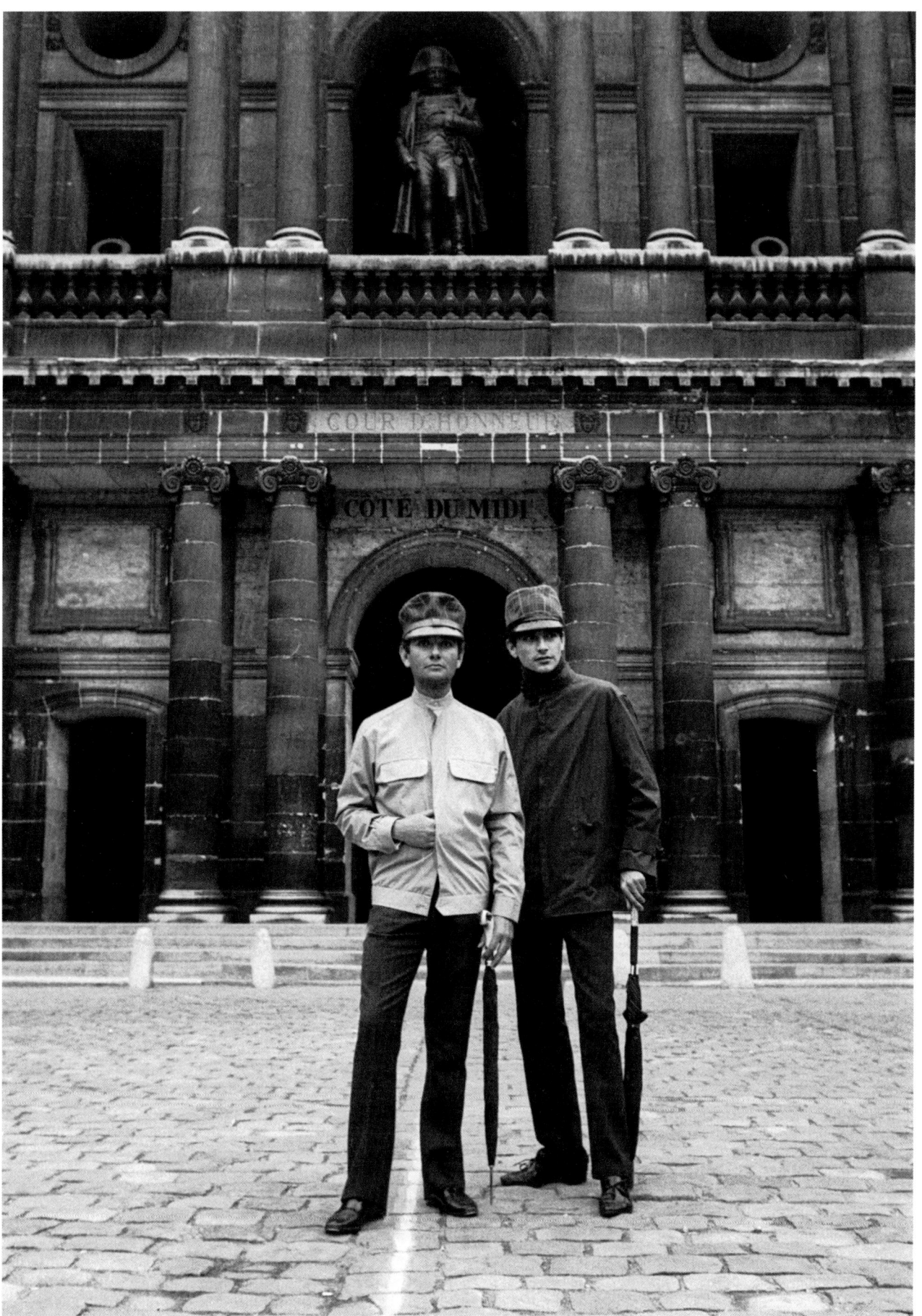

THE 1960s

This was the decade when, propelled by the Cold War, outer space invaded people's homes through the television set via a series of unforgettable images. Pierre paid tribute to the giants of this new era with his "Cosmos" line, which was both functional and comfortable.

His success was on a worldwide scale. He launched the licensing system, which was also a total success. People were proud to wear the Pierre Cardin label in couture and ready-to-wear alike. Pierre often said: "Without ready-to-wear, there would be no couturier." The same fashion designers who once mocked him were now following in his footsteps.

Until this point, children had been seen as "adults in miniature." The "Trente Glorieuses" gave them an image of their own: "juniors" were now having a moment. Western society was getting younger, children's status was changing, and social relationships were relaxing. Once again, Pierre braced for a new challenge: the creation of "Cardin Junior," in 1968, a highly symbolic year in France. The press and posters of Paris showcased young models elegantly dressed in Pierre Cardin. Riding yet another wave of success, Pierre went a step further: he set out to find triplets, dress them from head to foot, and turn them into models. He ended up with two hundred of them, whom he showcased here and there in reports and advertising. He now had the press at his feet.

Model Maggi Eckardt wears a suit over a wool cashmere-printed bodysuit, haute couture Fall–Winter 1964–65 collection. Photograph by Richard Dormer for *Harper's Bazaar*, September 1964.

Presentation of a set of designs from the haute couture Fall–Winter 1963–64 collection at the Saint-Ouen flea market. Photograph by Paul Huf.

Left:
Model Monique Chevalier wears a double-breasted, trapeze woolen coat from the Spring–Summer 1960 collection. Photograph by Mark Shaw.

Facing page:
A mohair coat with a curved collar, closed by a large leather belt, a creation by Pierre Cardin for the New York fashion house Zelinka-Matlick. Photograph by Irving Penn for *Vogue*, February 15, 1963.

Facing page:
Siv Benno in a rectangular-backed cocktail dress and Pierre Hogard in a tuxedo, in front of the spectacular panoramic view of Notre-Dame de Paris from the restaurant La Tour d'Argent. Photograph from 1962, by Franz Christian Gundlach.

Above:
At the Drugstore Publicis in 1960, a balloon coat with double-pleated sleeves. Photograph by Willy Maywald, who appears in the mirror behind the bar.

Making Fashion Modern

Above:
Model Karin Mossberg photographed in 1966 by Franz Christian Gundlach in a tartan suit cut on the bias with a fox-trimmed hood.

Facing page:
Hiroko under the porch at 118 Rue du Faubourg Saint-Honoré. She wears a white wool coat with a fox-trimmed porthole hat. Fall–Winter collection 1966–67. Photograph by Yoshi Takata.

Facing page:
Articulated sculpture necklace in steel plate and resin, 1968.

Above:
Maryse Gaspard, star model and muse of Pierre Cardin from 1966, in a crepe evening dress with a steel sculpture necklace set with a diamond. Spring–Summer 1968 collection.

Page 183:
The model wears a wool tube coat belted at the waist, with knife pleat collar and cuffs.

Making Fashion Modern

"What is asked of a great designer is not to create a beautiful, tailored, well-made dress. A fashion designer is asked to modify the face of the world through the structure of the piece, by the cut and by the line."

Pierre Cardin, interview with Claude Lanzmann, Dim Dam Dom, *ORTF, May 12, 1968.*

Facing page:
Sleeveless belted suit, photographed in 1960 by Guy Bourdin.

Right:
Model Carla Marlier wears a blouson-back coat with a box pleat from the haute couture Fall–Winter 1963–64 collection. Photograph by Guy Arsac.

Page 186:
The futuristic lines of the Cosmocorps collection are in perfect harmony with those of the roof of the Paris Observatory. Photograph by Franz Christian Gundlach.

Page 187:
Model Cathee Dahmen wears a herringbone coat with leather inlay and an aviator helmet, haute couture Fall–Winter 1968–69 collection. Photo by Antonio Miralda, published in *Elle*, August 26, 1968.

JEANNE MOREAU, THE MUSE

Pierre Cardin had a complicated personal life. He was profoundly attached to André Oliver but, in his forties, the desire for a child started to take hold. He met Jeanne Moreau through the world of cinema. The actress was trying to acquire a piece by Gabrielle Chanel and used the occasion to ask the designer to make her costumes for the film *Eva* by Joseph Losey. Unable to satisfy the needs of the star, the couturière suggested she go to Pierre Cardin instead. Since Jeanne had a model figure, Pierre's clothes fit her like a dream—and she fell madly in love with him, pursuing him until he too was smitten. The actress even expressed a wish to re-marry. Her knight in shining armor, the iconic fashion designer was perturbed about their common desire for a child. "She wanted to get married, but you know, it's best to be wary about unions with actors," he said.

The paparazzi harassed the legendary couple. As Pierre put it (words later quoted in *Le Figaro-Madame* on December 30, 2020), "I could have [had a child]. I had the mother, Jeanne [Moreau]. I was the one who refused. I was very seductive, young, not bad-looking, which served me well by the way. But I was always a gentleman. I didn't want to be Monsieur Moreau and she couldn't have played Madame Cardin. It was probably some kind of foolish pride."

The designer liked to say that the two of them chose each other, caught up in a love-at-first-sight experience worthy of a fairytale. "We were both successful. Our mantra: respect each other, never step on each other's toes or get embroiled in each other's business. We had to remain independent at all costs."

Jeanne was six years younger than the designer and beautiful, with a brilliant acting career. She represented a kind of ideal of the French woman. The question begged itself: should the two take their relationship to the next level? Pierre saw himself above all as a creator, an artist, and a businessman. He chose work as the guiding light of his life, rather than family. The love story would end four years later, ushering in a period of darkness and sorrow. Jeanne got sick. Despite their painful parting, the two ultimately remained friends, honoring and preserving what was left of their relationship.

Jeanne Moreau and Pierre Cardin. The actress wears a white brocade silk coat with a fox fur collar.

Above:
Pierre Cardin and
Jeanne Moreau at a dance
party at the Eiffel Tower
in November 1961 to
celebrate the 352nd
production of Marcel
Achard's play *L'idiote*.
Marcel and Juliette
Achard were close friends
of Pierre Cardin.

Facing page:
Fitting in the couture
salons. Jeanne Moreau
wears a cocktail dress
with a knotted collar
and mink cuffs.

"She was beautiful, just as I imagined beauty should be. She corresponded to what I had in mind: sensitive, intelligent—transcendent.

Pierre Cardin, "Jeanne Moreau et Pierre Cardin, les amants immortels," interview with Henry-Jean Servat, Paris Match, *January 11, 2001.*

The actress in 1961 photographed by Georges Dambier during the photo shoot for the cover of the album *Jeanne Moreau chante Bassiak.*

Above:
Pierre Cardin would say that Jeanne Moreau was exceptionally attractive. "She never infringed upon my career in fashion and I never did in her career, whether it be on the stage or in the cinema. We had mutual respect for each other, that's what created our great bond."

Facing page:
Jeanne Moreau in Joseph Losey's *Eva*, 1962. Dressed by Cardin, she is wearing a leather coat with a fur collar.

In 1964, Jeanne Moreau posed for *Paris Match* in Pierre Cardin's salon, wearing an embroidered silk crepe cocktail dress, with Voyou, the designer's poodle.

A SELF-MADE MAN

From an entrepreneurial point of view, Pierre Cardin saw himself as an unapologetic capitalist. At the same time, he called himself a socialist, because he claimed to work "for others" and even "in the service of others." He always considered himself a self-made man, who built a commercial and industrial empire from scratch. He knew how to bring his boat safely to harbor, to see things through—a rare quality indeed.

The personal image he cultivated was soon influenced by the cosmos, satellites, scientists, and lasers—all real sources of inspiration. He wanted to create not just images, but images of the future. In this sense, he will always be a true seer. In the sixties, he sought to be different, to invent his own style. Some women were afraid of being mocked for wearing Pierre Cardin, but this period is now seen as defining the times. What used to be considered absurd, unconscionable, insolent, or unwearable we now see—twenty-five years later—as what was actually being worn at the time: a detail that makes all the difference.

When it came to money matters, Pierre pursued his personal course: investing money was the key to opening up new possibilities. He would develop and enrich these "possibilities" in two directions: culture and furniture.

Pierre Cardin in 1975 in his apartment, in front of a lacquer and embroidered silk screen from the Imperial Palace in Tokyo. Shortly after this photograph was published in the press, the apartment was broken into and the pair of candle holders stolen.

Above:
Pierre Cardin
with Yoshi Takata
and Michael Lonsdale,
at a reception given
in honor of actress
Anna Magnani after
her triumph in *La Lupa*,
in June 1965.

Facing page:
The couturier in the large
salon of his apartment.

"A style is not born.
It's the original,
unique expression
of a personality
that itself evolves.
Style is a driving force,
ceaselessly modern,
in a world which, like
fashion, constantly
reinvents itself."

Pierre Cardin, "Je suis un Sisyphe heureux," Revue des Deux Mondes, *January 1993.*

Yves Saint Laurent
and Pierre Cardin.
Photograph taken
by Willy Rizzo in 1965.

Pierre Cardin poses in front of the large window of his salon in 1972. In the foreground, a fiberglass armchair by Mario Sabot.

"I can sleep
in Cardin beds,
sit in Cardin armchairs,
eat in Cardin dining
rooms, light my house,
go to the theater
or an exhibition, and
never leave my empire."

Pierre Cardin, in Benjamin Loyauté, Pierre Cardin Evolution. Furniture and Design, *Éditions Flammarion, Style & Design Collection, 2006.*

Left:
Prototypes of the "Espace" secretary and chair in carved wood before a black lacquer coating was added. Design by François Cante-Pacos for Pierre Cardin, c. 1972–73.

Facing page:
Pierre Cardin poses in front of the "Insect" vanity table in black laminate with circular doors and drawers that open remotely, 1978–79.

Above:
The West Wind 1124 aircraft designed entirely by the Pierre Cardin Design Studio for Atlantic Aviation in 1978.

Facing page:
Pierre Cardin was the first designer to be featured on the cover of *Time* magazine, for the December 23, 1974 issue. Photograph by Eddie Adams.

A MAN OF CULTURE

Fuelled by a permanent and insatiable curiosity, on January 1, 1970, Pierre Cardin became the manager of the Ambassadeurs theater and restaurant just off the Champs-Élysées. He immediately made his mark, transforming the interior architecture and promoting a resolutely contemporary cultural program spanning music, dance, theater, painting, sculpture, literature, cinema, and photography. He created an astonishingly dynamic venue, whose prestige extended well beyond the borders of France. The Espace Cardin was a ship of dreams moored right near the Seine and known to all Paris connoisseurs. It had a dream location, not far from the Cours la Reine promenade, on the city's Right Bank, and the Quai d'Orsay, set across the Seine on the Left Bank. Once again, Pierre Cardin had managed to set up shop in one of the most beautiful spots in the French capital. The Espace would go on to serve as a theater, screening venue, gallery, convention hall, and site for fashion shows and musical performances, as well as hosting conferences, auctions, and exhibitions. Known for showcasing dazzling artistic talent, it would gain recognition far and wide.

Pierre still harbored a long unfulfilled dream of becoming an actor, singer, or dancer—a desire revealing his taste for performance—something applauded at the time by Paris intellectuals and the cultivated elite. But among guardians of the bastion of order, it was more complicated: France likes to pigeonhole things.

A fashion designer in the theater? How absurd! Pierre was the butt of many jokes. "What a strange idea, Pierre Cardin in the theater. He excels in fashion; what on earth is he up to with this adventure?" He was going to show them, with beauty and grace, that the arts are all inextricably linked.

Another sector where Pierre Cardin's signature and style would shine through was furniture. Starting the same year, 1970, he began to create utilitarian, sculptural furniture for private clients before marketing it more broadly. It was one of his close friends, Maurice Rheims, a writer and auctioneer, who encouraged and advised him in this new endeavor.

Pierre Cardin at the Espace Cardin, in 1971.

Making Fashion Modern

Pierre Cardin posing in February 1976 in front of the former Théâtre des Ambassadeurs on Avenue Gabriel in Paris, which became the Espace Cardin, a cultural venue. The logo behind the designer was designed by François Cante-Pacos.

Making Fashion Modern

Above:
Among the many avant-garde performances programmed at the Espace Cardin, *The Prologue to Deafman Glance* by Bob Wilson, on May 28, 1971.

Right:
The Espace Cardin included a theater, restaurant, gallery, and four-hundred-seat cinema designed by Francesco Bocola, 1972–73.

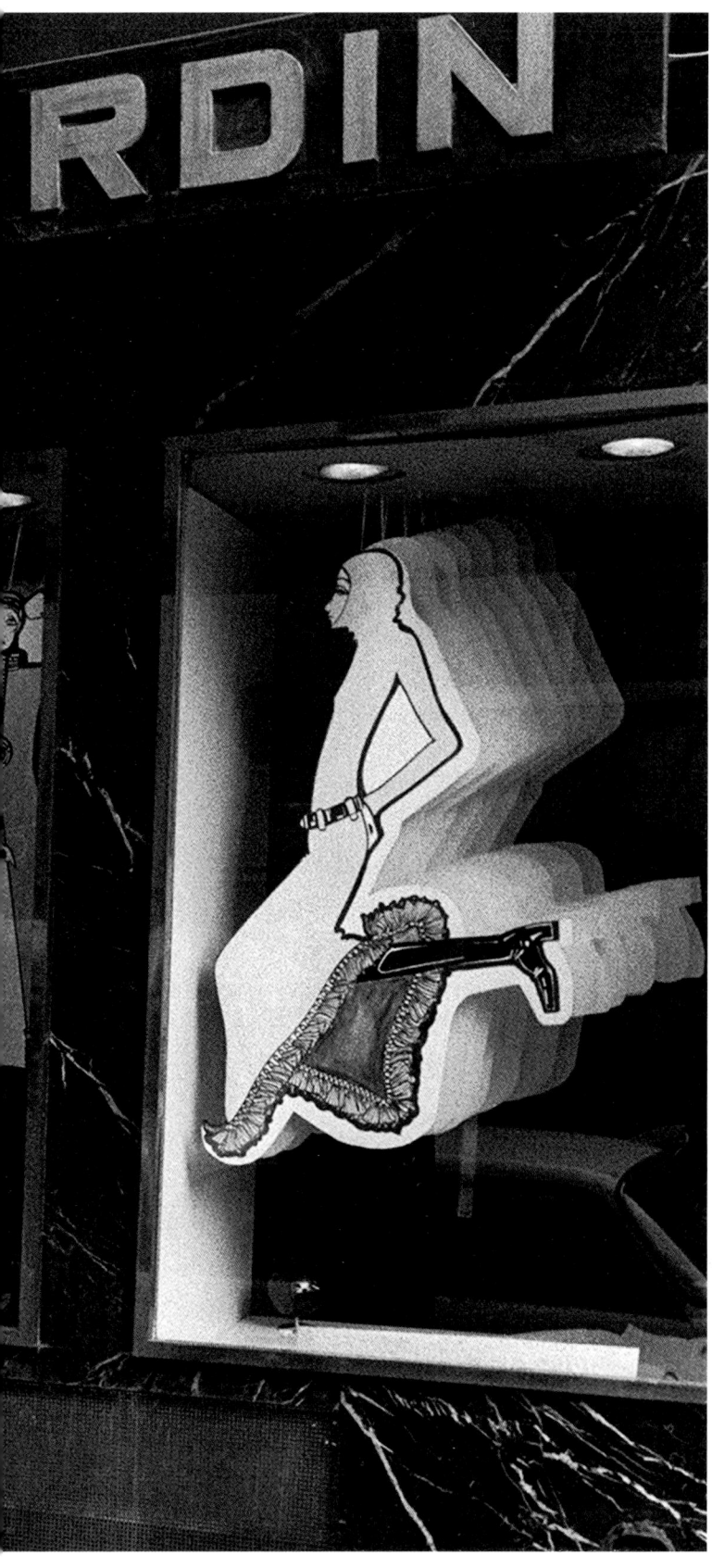

Posing in front of the boutique in a Cosmocorps suit, François-Marie Banier was Pierre Cardin's press officer from 1966 onwards.

THE COSMOCORPS ERA

Pierre Cardin always strived to create the images of tomorrow. He said he was influenced by the art and culture of the past, such as painting, but his inspiration came from many eclectic sources. An object, a situation, a photo could trigger a flash of inspiration and creativity. But the cosmos and lasers also had this power. The "average" person sees things, but the artist projects themselves onto them.

Pierre saw each garment as a vessel. Just as water is shapeless, he disregarded the chest or waist that would inhabit his creations, stepped back from the body and its representations. By relying on the line of a garment, he tried to highlight color first and foremost, since it is the first thing that people notice. Color, form, material: this was the holy trinity of creativity.

On the sixtieth anniversary of the opening of his fashion house, Pierre told *Express* that the "Cosmocorps," a unisex suit created in 1968, was the piece he was most proud of. A garment which did not sell much but was much talked about. Astronomy and the conquest of space entered the living rooms of ordinary people who had become spectators of their own daily lives. Pierre Cardin was fascinated. If the Cold War produced images that quickly became iconic, his Cosmos line would be an avant-garde tribute to the explorers of outer space. With this new line, Pierre Cardin paid homage to all those who were ready for the adventure of a fast-changing world. The most immediately striking thing about the collection: the wholly innovative lines, and the metallic look that seems the stuff of science fiction. It is the triumph of the "space age," with a unisex suit as the starlet—a bold attack on gender!

In the spring of 1967, the Cosmocorps was a key feature of Pierre's new collection with its flared, brightly colored clothes and the Pierre Cardin logo plastered everywhere. Birdcage helmets and waists encircled by wide leather belts also featured. Women's magazines acclaimed the collection and the public soon followed suit. *Elle* immediately recognized it as a watershed moment. Within a few days, the weekly fashion magazine had organized a major photo shoot in its studios.

A coat with silver plastic collar and cuffs, 1966. Photograph by Yoshi Takata.

Making Fashion Modern

The figures speak for themselves: no less than sixty-five technicians and assistants, and five photographers, shot for eighteen hours straight, yielding some three thousand photographs. New, sometimes crazy, ideas were flying around like mad. The avant-garde had become the norm. Alas, this formidable wave of the too-new would not be fully harnessed, though the whirlwind left no one indifferent.

The house of Pierre Cardin was vindicated fifty years later when it successfully launched the Cosmocorps 3022 collection, a major fashion show inspired by the conquest of space, at the Musée de l'Air et de l'Espace (Air and Space Museum) in Le Bourget. The new manager of the brand, Rodrigo Basilicati-Cardin, evoked on this occasion "a year's efforts in perfect continuity with Pierre Cardin's work," and illustrating the inimitable Cardin touch.

Many couturiers and fashion designers have tried their whole lives to serve the body, the arts, fashion, and beauty. Pierre Cardin alone has succeeded in carrying out this mission. His sense of aesthetics allowed him to invent, to seek, to create beauty his whole life long. But he also had a real sense of duty and felt that it was his obligation to succeed. Perhaps he spent his life looking for the lost sensuality and comfort the small white coat of his childhood had given him. He felt that he was somehow "the chosen one." He sensed that this was his calling: to dress and embellish others, both ordinary people and the stars, and thus to embellish life itself.

The quality of a work of art is often measured several years, decades or centuries after it is made by how well it withstands the test of time. Especially if it continues to provoke emotion. So it will be with Pierre Cardin's oeuvre—at once beautiful, innovative, inventive and moving. Without a doubt, Pierre is the artist who has gone the furthest in blurring the lines between life and work.

On December 29, 2020, after a lifetime of hard work and success, Pierre Cardin passed away. He leaves behind an empire, but, above all, the indelible mark of his visions and his exacting standards. His was a life most only ever dream of. More than any one singular creation, his lasting legacy is his taste for originality, simplicity, elegance, and modernity.

Provocative and visionary, the faux-fur coats of the Fall–Winter 1969–70 collection. Photograph by Yoshi Takata.

"I seek my inspirations neither in the past, nor in the great book of fashion, nor in the work of other designers. Only the present interests me. I've always had this innate faculty to foresee and create clothes that never existed and that adapt to the psychological and scientific progress of our time: cellular biology, kinetic fashion, computing, the space adventure."

Pierre Cardin, *"Je suis un Sisyphe heureux,"* Revue des Deux Mondes, *January 1993.*

The bold thermoformed dresses baptized Cardines, worn with hats, gloves, and vinyl over-the-knee boots, 1968.

Left:
The conquest of space has fed the imagination of popular culture, and that of Pierre Cardin. A recent pastiche of a comic book, *Space Girls*, is directly inspired by the designer's futurist fashion and visionary ideas.

Facing page:
A flap skirt worn over a bodysuit and vinyl necklace, 1968.

"I had the chance to discover his incomparable savoir faire while posing for him, very young, as a model. Our connection was unexplainable, we could understand each other without words, simply through a look. From the young country girl that I was, he managed to create a modern woman."

Maryse Gaspard, 2022.

Maryse Gaspard, in a long woolen dress with multicolored square inlays, Fall–Winter 1967–68 collection. Maryse was the star fitting model of the Cardin house from 1966. The designer loved to create for her form. She accompanied him on all his trips abroad and was appointed Director of Haute Couture in the late 1970s.

Above:
The Cosmocorps line, presented at the foot of the Eiffel Tower, in 1968.

Facing page:
A striped woolen ensemble presented at the Espace Cardin.

Above:
Zipped coats in thick printed wool with giant polka dots hemmed with fox fur, 1968.

Facing page:
The typical silhouette of the Cosmocorps line, a short sleeveless wool dress, tightly belted, worn with a helmet hat and stockings of the same color, a design inspired by the world of science fiction for the Fall–Winter 1967–68 collection.

"I do not know how to describe his form of intelligence, his imagination. He thinks like an engineer, but is not an engineer. He's afraid of nothing, nothing is too much for him. If he could open something on the moon, he would do it!"

Claude Brouet in "Pierre Cardin, l'éternel futur," Vanity Fair, December 29, 2020.

David Tollame in a dinner jacket and Hiroko in silk gazar evening wear.

"It's the line, and only the line, that interests me. That is what I did for the first time: present male styles as if they were a fashion—as a line. No padding, no stiffening, the suit close to the body but supple, the sleeves narrow, the shoulders respected but unexaggerated, the collar low so you don't have that disgraceful wrinkle at the neck, the pants narrow, accentuating the thin, flat look."

Pierre Cardin, "La Mode Masculine," New York Times, *April 21, 1968.*

The female model wears a silk crepe evening gown trimmed with brown mink, while Gilles Laugier models a suit from the Cosmocorps line. Photograph by Yoshi Takata, 1966.

"I have always very much admired this enigmatic and fascinating man. A man of paradoxes and contradictions in his designs just as in his personal life. A man with neither boundaries, nor limits, whether they are creative or imposed. A man for whom the present is the future."

Marisa Berenson, in Jean-Pascal Hesse, Pierre Cardin, *Assouline, 2017.*

Marisa Berenson in an embroidered evening gown from the Spring–Summer 1967 collection. Photograph by Irving Penn for *Vogue*, September 1967.

"The woman is
a kind of flower that
later comes into its own.
I draw vases.
Shapes guide me.
A woman is fluid,
she is like water that flows
into the shapes I create."

Pierre Cardin, "Je suis un Sisyphe heureux," Revue des Deux Mondes, *January 1993.*

Model Editha Düssler in a crepe and ostrich feather evening gown from the haute couture Fall–Winter 1965–66 collection. Photograph by Henry Clarke.

Left:
Long evening gown in double orange nylon gabardine, from the haute couture Spring–Summer 1970 collection. Photograph by Richard Dormer.

Facing page:
Model Susan von Haaren in a reversible woolen evening coat with bow closure, haute couture Fall–Winter 1970–71 collection. Photograph by Neal Barr.

"The garment I prefer is the one I invent for a life that does not exist yet, the world of tomorrow."

Pierre Cardin, Vogue Paris, *December 30, 2020.*

Zipped bodysuit with helmet, vest, and vinyl leather posing pouch, 1968.

A fashion show of the Cosmocorps collection in front of the boutique at 118 Rue du Faubourg Saint-Honoré, in 1969. The models are dressed in sleeveless, zipped vinyl tunics.

A presentation
of accessories and belts
at the Espace Cardin.

Right:
A wool bolero dress
with quilted neckline
photographed
at the Espace Cardin
by Franz Christian
Gundlach, 1970.

Pages 248–49:
The only boutique
opened by Pierre Cardin
on the Left Bank,
Boulevard Saint-Germain,
during the events of 1968.

Yoshi Takata was a mysterious woman—discreet, hidden behind dark glasses.
Pierre Cardin's creative partner for over fifty years, Mademoiselle Takata, as we used to
call her, was a passionate and esteemed photographer.
At her side, I learned to look differently at both photography and life in general. Her
curiosity, her passion for art, and her taste as an eccentric collector have deeply inspired me.
Until the very end, she was a modern, original, and iconoclastic woman: a true adventurer.

I thank her for sharing with me the wonders of her unique perspective.

Pierre Pelegry

Yoshi Takata photographied by Martine Franck.

Acknowledgments

First and foremost, we thank Suzanne Tise-Isoré for accompanying, supporting, and counselling us during all the stages of this book.
We would also like to thank the entire Flammarion team for helping us undertake this work, in particular Karine Huguenaud, Clément Prats, Lara Lo Calzo, Virginie Picat, and Loïc Derrien.

Thank you to Jean Paul Gaultier for his foreword and for his unfailing loyalty to Pierre Cardin.

We also extend our sincere gratitude to Marie-Noëlle de Vassal for her welcome and generous contribution.

For their participation and availability, we extend our warmest thanks to Rodrigo Basilicati-Cardin, Renée Taponier, Maryse Gaspard, Mélanie Bouexiere, and Oto Kveselava.

Finally, for their precious help, Michael Berger-Sandhofer, Marisa Berenson, Laura Bertaux, Bruno Biagi, Olivier Bialobos, Frédéric Bourdelier, Morgane Brossard, Claude Brouet, Quentin Carvalo, Bernard Danillon, Guillaume Dambier, Annie and Jean Frachon, Bruno Fray, Sebastian Lux, Charles Maze, Volker Marschall, Jutta Niemann, Pierre Passebon, Audrey Pelegry, Thaddaeus Ropac, Francesco Rossetti, Arthur de Vassal, Éric Vibart, Patrick Sanois, Jasmin Seck, Céleste Trétout, and Xavier Lacaille.

A very special thank-you to my friend Danielle Cillien-Sabatier for always encouraging and counselling me.

Pierre Cardin once gave me this picture as a gift. It is the perfect illustration of a certain idea of happiness. We see him here smiling with André Oliver in Port La Galère. I am forever indebted to him for his trust during all the years I spent by his side.

Jean-Pascal Hesse

Index

Page numbers in italic correspond to captions; page numbers in bold correspond to quotations:

A
Achard, Juliette *190*
Achard, Marcel *190*
Adams, Eddie *208*
Agnelli, Gianni *142*
Aillencourt, Simone d' *58*
Aimée, Anouk *132*
Alphand, Hervé 128, *141*
Alphand, Nicole 128, *141*
Arc, Joan of 19
Arenberg, Prince of *52*
Arnaud, Marie-Hélène *70, 86*
Arsac, Guy *185*
Auclair, Michel 31
Avedon, Richard 108
Aviliers, Baroness of 65

B
Bacall, Lauren 128, *147*
Balenciaga, Cristóbal 58
Banier, François-Marie *217*
Bardot, Brigitte *130,* 139
Barr, Neal *240*
Barrault, Jean-Louis 12
Basilicati-Cardin, Rodrigo 221
Beaumont, Étienne de 46
Beatles, The 8, 139, 155, 161, *161*
Bécaud, Gilbert *147*
Beistegui, Charles de 46, *52*
Benno, Siv *177*
Bérard, Christian 28, 30–31, *33–35*, 38
Berenson, Marisa **237**, *237*
Berghauer, Henri 108
Blanguernon, Karen *91*
Bocola, Francesco *214*
Bogart, Leslie 128
Bompuis, Louis 19, 20
Boubat, Édouard *13*
Bourdin, Guy *185*
Bousquet, Marie-Louise 58
Boussac, Marcel 31, 44
Brandolini d'Adda, Countess Cristiana *142*
Bricard, Mizza 32, *38*
Brissac, Duchess of *52*
Brouet, Claude **232**
Brynner, Doris *49*
Buffet, Annabel (born Schwob de Lure) *123, 125, 147*
Buffet, Bernard *123, 125, 126, 142, 147*
Bukowa, Angelica Lazansky von *120*

C
Callas, Maria 31, *120, 123*
Cante-Pacos, François *206, 212*
Cardin, Alba 18
Cardin, Alessandro 16, 35
Cardin, Maria 16, 18
Cardin, Palmira 18
Cardin, Rita 18
Cardin, Teresa 18
Carré, Marguerite 32
Cartier-Bresson, Henri *13*

Cartier, Jacques 121
Castillo, Antonio del 28
Chanel, Gabrielle 20, 188
Charlemagne 19
Chevalier, Monique *174*
Clarke, Henry *238*
Clément, René 31
Cocteau, Jean 11, 28, 30–31, *31*
Columbus, Christopher 121

D
Dahl-Wolfe, Louise *34*
Dahmen, Cathee *185*
Dambier, Georges *58, 70, 75, 86, 91, 192*
Darnand, Joseph 23
Davis Jr., Sammy *137,* 155
Day, Josette 33
Delannoy, Jean 31
Delrieu, Hélène *70*
Delubac, Jacqueline *142*
Depardieu, Gérard 139
Dietrich, Marlène 139
Dillmann de Jarnac, Isabelle **130**
Dior, Christian 11, 24, 31–32, 34–38, *34, 38,* 44, 46, *52,* 58, 118
Doisneau, Robert *13*
Dormer, Richard *170, 240*
Düssler, Editha *238*
Dutronc, Jacques *135,* 155

E
Eckardt, Maggi *170*
Epstein, Brian *38,* 161
Escoffier, Auguste 28
Escoffier, Marcel 28, 30–31, 44

F
Fairchild, John *100*
Farrow, Mia *132,* 139
Fiedler, Christa *181*
Fitzgerald, Ella 139
Franck, Martine *250*
François, Claude 155

G
Gaspard, Maryse 12, *181,* **226**, *226*
Gaulle, Charles de 128
Giraudoux, Jean 35
Givenchy, Hubert de 58
Godard, Jean-Luc *92*
Graziani, Bettina *75*
Grès, Madame 65
Guitry, Sacha 31
Gundlach, Franz Christian *177–178, 185, 246*

H
Haaren, Susan von *240*
Halliday, Johnny 155
Hammond, Celia *4*
Hammond, Harry *161*
Handke, Peter 139

Hardy, Françoise *147*
Hayworth, Rita *46*
Henry, Pierre *8*
Hepburn, Audrey *139*
Hériat, Philippe *32*
Hesse, Jean-Pascal **237**
Horst, Horst P. *26*
Huf, Paul *173*

J
Jacques, Christian *44*
James, Charles **62**
Jarre, Jean-Michel *8*

K
Kammerman, Eugène *38*
Karina, Anna *91*
Kazan, Lionel *150*
Kennedy, Jacqueline (born Bouvier) *128, 141*

L
La Cambredette, Countess of *24, 26*
Lamorisse, Lucien *65*
Lanzmann, Claude **182**
Lanzmann, Jacques *135*
Laroche, Guy *118*
Laugier, Gilles *234*
Lazareff, Hélène *58*
Lazareff, Pierre *58*
Léaud, Jean-Pierre *108*
Leigh, Vivien *46*
Lelong, Lucien *31, 32, 65*
Liptnitski, Boris *35*
Lonsdale, Michaël *200*
López Willshaw, Arturo *58*
López Willshaw, Patricia *49*
Losey, Joseph *44, 188, 194*
Louis XIV (king of France) *19*

M
Macnee, Patrick *161*
Magnani, Anna *200*
Marais, Jean *31, 31, 33*
Marlier, Carla *185*
Martine, Franck *250*
Matsumoto, Hiroko *100, 108, 108, 114, 178, 232*
Maywald, Willy *36, 91, 177*
McCartney, Paul *161*
McCartney, Stella *161*
Millings, Douglas *161*
Moral, Jean *35*
Moreau, Jeanne *11, 188, 188, 190, **192**, 192, 194, 196*
Mossberg, Karin *178*
Munch, Charles *155*
Mussolini, Benito *18*

N
Napoleon I (emperor of France) *19, 168*
Nehru, Jawaharlal *161*
Newton, Helmut *108*
Nixon, Patricia *142*
Nixon, Richard *142*

O
Obaldia, Diane de *65*
Oliver, André *12, 65, 80, 116, 126, 128, 142, 147, 188, 251*
Ophüls, Max *44*

Oppenheimer, Walter *58*
Ostier, André *49*

P
Paquin, Jeanne *28*
Parkinson, Norman *4, 76*
Pasolini, Pier Paolo *12*
Pasteur, Louis *19*
Paulvé, André *31*
Penn, Irving *174, 237*
Perón, Eva *58*
Philippe, Gérard *46*
Polo, Marco *96*
Popesco, Elvire *46*
Popinat, Blanche *20*
Pottier, Philippe *55*

R
Radziwill, Lee (born Bouvier) *141*
Redé, Baron de (Alexis von Rosenberg) *49, 58*
Régy, Claude *12*
Rheims, Maurice *210*
Rigg, Diana *161*
Rizzo, Willy *202*
Rolling Stones, The *155*

S
Saad, Georges *255*
Saint Laurent, Yves *24, 118, 202*
Schiaparelli, Elsa *26, 31*
Schlebrügge, Nena von *76*
Servat, Henry-Jean **192**
Shaw, Mark *44, 60, 174*
Sinatra, Frank *132*
Smith, Jimmy *142, 155*
Snow, Carmel *37, 58*
Spencer, Lady Raine *58*

T
Takata, Yoshi *8, 11–13, 13–14, 78, 96, 102, 106, 123, 128, 141–142, 155, 178, 200, 214, 218, 221, 234, 250, 250, 255*
Taylor, Elizabeth *128, 139*
Terzieff, Laurent *130*
Thurman, Uma *76*
Tollame, David *232*
Truffaut, François *108*

V
Vassal, Roland de *6, 11, 11, 65–66, 70, 75, 78, 86, 114, 155, 161, 165*
Vercingetorix (Gallic chieftain) *19*
Visconti, Luchino *11, 31, 44*

W
Waltener, Monsieur *24, 26*
Ward, Christopher *168*
Warwick, Dionne *128, 139*
Welch, Raquel *128*
Westminster, Duchess of *58*
Wilson, Bob *12, 214*
Windsor, Duchess of *102*
Worth, Charles Frederick *65*

Z
Zeffirelli, Franco *31*
Zehnacker, Raymonde *32*
Zola, Émile *121*

Photographic Credits

t: top, b: bottom

All photographs in this book were provided by Archives Pierre Cardin except for those on the following pages:
Front cover: © Norman Parkinson/Iconic Images; back cover: © Archives Roland de Vassal; p. 2: © Ullstein bild Dtl./Ullstein bild via Getty Images; pp. 5–7: © Archives Roland de Vassal; p. 9: © Yoshi Takata/Courtesy of Pierre Pelegry; p. 10: © Archives Roland de Vassal; p. 13: © All rights reserved; pp. 14–15: Yoshi Takata/Courtesy of Pierre Pelegry; p. 27: © Courtesy of Paci Contemporary gallery (Brescia–Porto Cervo, IT) and Horst Estate/Condé Nast; p. 29: © Photo12/ABC/Lionel Hahn; p. 30: © Adagp/Comité Cocteau, Paris 2022/© Cecil Beaton Archive/Condé Nast; p. 33t: © Glasshouse Images/Photo12/André Paulvé; p. 33b: © Sunset Boulevard/Corbis Historical via Getty Images; p. 34: © Louise Dahl-Wolfe Archive/Center for Creative Photography, Arizona Board of Regents; p. 35: © Boris Lipnitzki/Roger-Viollet; p. 36: © Association Willy Maywald/Adagp, 2022; Paris; p. 38: © Collection Dior Héritage, Paris. All rights reserved; p. 39: © Archives Charmet/Bridgeman Images; pp. 40–41: © Pat English/The Life Picture Collection/Shutterstock; pp. 42–43: Eugene Kammerman/Gamma-Rapho; p. 45: © Mark Shaw/Mptvimages.com; p. 46: © Archives Roland de Vassal; p. 47: Yoshi Takata/courtesy of Pierre Pelegry; p. 48: © All rights reserved; pp. 49–51: © Association André Ostier; p. 55: Philippe Pottier; p. 56: © Mattia Aquila; p. 57: © Archives Roland de Vassal; p. 59: Georges Dambier; p. 60: © Archives Roland de Vassal; p. 61: © Mark Shaw/Mptvimages.com; pp. 63–64: © Archives Roland de Vassal; pp. 66-67: © Archives Roland de Vassal; p. 69: © Archives Roland de Vassal; pp. 70–71: © Georges Dambier; p. 72–74: © Archives Roland de Vassal; p. 75: © Georges Dambier; pp. 76–77: © Norman Parkinson/Iconic Images; pp. 80–81: © Yoshi Takata/Courtesy of Pierre Pelegry; pp. 82–85: © Archives Roland de Vassal; pp. 86–87: © Georges Dambier; pp. 88–89: © Archives Roland de Vassal; pp. 90–91: © Georges Dambier; p. 92: © All rights reserved; p. 93: © Archives Roland de Vassal; p. 94: © Association Willy Maywald/ADAGP, Paris 2022; p. 95: © Georges Dambier; pp. 101–11: © Yoshi Takata/Courtesy of Pierre Pelegry; p. 112: © Archives Roland de Vassal; p. 113: © Yoshi Takata/Courtesy of Pierre Pelegry; p. 114: © Pierluigi Praturlon; pp. 116–17: © Giancarlo Botti/Gamma Rapho; p. 119: © Henri Elwing/Hprints; p. 120: © Giancarlo Botti/Gamma-Rapho; p. 122: © Yoshi Takata/Courtesy of Pierre Pelegry; pp. 124–25: © Reporters Associes/Gamma-Rapho via Getty Images; pp. 128–29: © Yoshi Takata/Courtesy of Pierre Pelegry; p. 131: © Leonard de Raemy/Sygma Premium via Getty Images; p. 132: © Giancarlo Botti/Gamma-Rapho; p. 133: © Bill Eppridge/THE LIFE Picture Collection/Shutterstock; pp. 134–35: © Jean-Claude Deutsch/Paris Match/Scoop; p. 136: © Giancarlo Botti/Gamma-Rapho; p. 137: © Giancarlo Botti/Gamma-Rapho; p. 138: © NBC Television/Hulton Archive via Getty Images; p. 140: © Yoshi Takata/Courtesy of Pierre Pelegry; p. 141t: © Keyston/Hulton Archive via Getty Images; pp. 141b–45: © Yoshi Takata/Courtesy of Pierre Pelegry; pp. 146–47: © CBS Photo Archive/Getty Images;

pp. 148–49: © All rights reserved; p. 151: © Lionel Kazan; pp. 152–53: © Yoshi Takata/Courtesy of Pierre Pelegry; pp. 156–57: © Reporters Associes/Gamma-Rapho via Getty Images; pp. 159-60: © Archives Roland de Vassal; p. 161: © Harry Hammond/V&A Images/Hulton Archive/Getty Images; p. 164: © Archives Roland de Vassal; p. 166: © Yoshi Takata/Courtesy of Pierre Pelegry; p. 167: © Doreen Spooner/Mirrorpix/Getty Images; p. 169: © Reporters Associes/Gamma-Rapho via Getty Images; p. 171: © Courtesy of Hearst Magazines UK; pp. 172–73: © Paul Huf; p. 174: © Mark Shaw/Mptvimages.com; p. 175: © Irving Penn, Vogue/Condé Nast; p. 176: © F. C. Gundlach; p. 177: © Association Willy Maywald/ADAGP, Paris 2022; p. 178: © F. C. Gundlach; p. 179: © Yoshi Takata/Courtesy of Pierre Pelegry; p. 180: © Jérôme Faggiano and Nils Herrmann; p. 181: © AP/SIPA; p. 184: © The Guy Bourdin Estate 2022, Courtesy of Louise Alexander Gallery, L'Officiel de la Couture et de la Mode, 1960; p. 185: © Guy Arsac, L'Officiel de la Couture et de la Mode, 1963; p. 186: © F. C. Gundlach; p. 187: © Antonio Miralda/ELLE France; p. 189: © All rights reserved; p. 190: © Patrice Habans/Paris Match/Scoop; p. 191: © Yoshi Takata/Courtesy of Pierre Pelegry; p. 193: © Georges Dambier; p. 194: © All rights reserved; p. 195: © Paris Film Productions/Interopa/Everett Collection/Aurimages; pp. 196–97: © François Pagès/Paris Match/Scoop; p. 199: © Gianni Girani/Reporters Associati & Archivi/Mondadori Portfolio Premium via Getty Images; p. 201: © Jean-Philippe Charbonnier/Gamma-Rapho; p. 203: Willy Rizzo, Paris-1965; p. 204: © Stills/Gamma-Rapho via Getty Images; p. 206: © Archives François Cante-Pacos; p. 207: © J. Cuinières; p. 208: © Archives François Cante-Pacos; p. 209: © Eddie Adams/Time Inc.; pp. 212–213: © Patrice Picot/Gamma-Rapho via Getty Images; p. 214: © Courtesy of Robert Wilson Archives and the Byrd Hoffman Water Mill Foundation; p. 215: © Yoshi Takata/Courtesy of Pierre Pelegry; pp. 216–17: © UPI/AFP; pp. 219–23: Yoshi Takata/Courtesy of Pierre Pelegry; p. 224: © @parsonsdropout; pp. 225–30: © Yoshi Takata/Courtesy of Pierre Pelegry; p. 231: © Patrick Rouchon/Akg-images; pp. 233–35: © Yoshi Takata/Courtesy of Pierre Pelegry; p. 236: © Irving Penn, Vogue/Condé Nast; p. 241: © Henry Clarke, Musée Galliera/ADAGP, Paris 2022/Dist. RMN-Grand Palais/Image ville de Paris; p. 240: © Richard Dormer; p. 239: © Neal Barr; p. 244: © Bettman via Getty Images; p. 245: © Yoshi Takata/Courtesy of Pierre Pelegry; pp. 246–47: © F. C. Gundlach; pp. 248–49: © Bettmann via Getty Images; p. 250: © Martine Franck/Magnum Photos; p. 256: © Georges Saad.

In reproducing the images featured in this publication, the publisher obtained the permission of the rights holders whenever possible. Should the publisher have been unable to locate the rights holders, notwithstanding good-faith efforts, it requests that any contact information concerning such rights holders be forwarded so that they may be contacted. Any errors or omissions referred to the publisher will be corrected in subsequent printings.

Page 256:
Pierre Cardin photographed by Georges Saad in the early 1960s.

Back cover:
Pierre Cardin in his couture salon at 118 Rue du Faubourg Saint-Honoré. Photograph by Roland de Vassal, 1958.